D1077630

THE OFFICIAL

THEORY TEST
for Car Drivers
and Motorcyclists

including the questions and answers
valid for tests taken from 28 July 1997

London: The Stationery Office

Written and compiled by the Publications Unit of the Driving Standards Agency

Questions and answers compiled by the National Foundation for Educational Research

Illustrations by Vicky Squires

The previous edition of this title was published by HMSO. This edition is published by The Stationery Office.

© Crown Copyright 1997
First published 1997
Reprinted 1997

Published with the permission of the Driving Standards Agency on behalf of the Controller of Her Majesty's Stationery Office

Applications for reproduction should be made in writing to The Copyright Unit, Her Majesty's Stationery Office, St Clements House, 2–16 Colegate, Norwich NR3 1BQ

First edition Crown copyright 1996

ISBN 0 11 551925 4

British Library Cataloguing in Publication Data
A CIP catalogue record for this book is available from the British Library

Acknowledgements

The Driving Standards Agency would like to thank the following for their assistance:

National Foundation for Educational Research

Transport Research Laboratory

Department of Transport

Driver and Vehicle Testing Agency, Northern Ireland

The staff of the Driving Standards Agency

Every effort has been made to ensure that the information contained in this publication is accurate at the time of going to press.
The Stationery Office cannot be held responsible for any inaccuracies.
Information in this book is for guidance only.

All metric and imperial conversions in this book are approximate.

DSA **THEORY TEST** for car drivers and m

The Driving Standards Agency (DSA) is an Exe[cutive]
of the Department of Transport. You'll see its l[ogo]

DRIVING
STANDARDS
AGENCY

'Safe driving for life'

The aim of DSA is to promote road safety throu[gh]
driving standards.

DSA

- conducts practical driving tests for drivers or [motorcyclists,]
  lorries, buses and other vehicles

- plans, maintains and supervises the theory tes[t for]
  motorcycles, lorries and buses

- controls the register of Approved Driving Inst[ructors]

- supervises Compulsory Basic Training (CBT)

- aims to provide a high-quality service to its cu[stomers]

DVTA

The Driver and Vehicle Tes[ting Agency]
is an Executive Agency wit[h the]
Environment for Northern [Ireland. Its aim]
is to promote and improve [the]
advancement of driving sta[ndards. As part]
of the Government's polici[es it tests the]
mechanical standards of ve[hicles.]

This book will help you to

- ▶ **study for your theory test**
- ▶ **prepare and help you to pass**

Part One gives you information on how to get started.

Part Two tells you about the question paper and how to answer it.

Part Three shows you the questions that may be used on your test. Don't worry, you won't have to answer all of them. Your paper will have 35 questions.

The questions are in the left-hand column with a choice of answers beneath. On the right of the page you'll find the correct answers and a brief explanation of why the answers are correct.

Books for study

Although this book helps to explain the answers, you should study other publications that cover the subjects in more detail. Buy and study a copy of *The Highway Code* (The Stationery Office). You can order one when you apply for your provisional licence or buy one from a newsagent or bookshop. DSA's *The Driving Manual* explains driving skills in more detail, and *Know Your Traffic Signs* is highly recommended (both published by The Stationery Office).

These books will help you to answer the questions correctly and will also guide you when studying for your practical test. Keep them so that you can refer to them throughout your driving life. You can find them in any good bookshop, together with relevant books from other publishers.

It's important that you study – not just to pass the test but to become a safe driver.

To ensure that all candidates are tested fairly, questions used in the theory test are under continuous review. A few of the questions used will be changed periodically to reflect changes in legislation, or as a result of customer feedback. If you take the theory test you may find questions that don't appear in this book. The information needed to answer them is readily available in the series of Driving Skills products and *The Highway Code*.

Driving is a life skill.

Your tests are just the beginning.

Some of the questions in this book give 'correct answers' that don't apply to Northern Ireland.

 These are marked with NI and an explanation is given in the text.

If you're a motorcycle rider there will be some specific questions on motorcycling. In this book those questions are marked with a motorcycle symbol.

If you want to drive a car

DSA approves instructors to teach learner drivers for payment. These instructors have their standards checked regularly.

Approved Driving Instructors (ADIs) must

- pass a difficult exam

- reach a high standard of instruction

- be registered with DSA or DVTA

- display an Approved Driving Instructor's certificate (except in Northern Ireland).

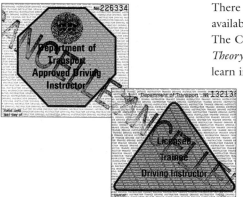

These professional instructors will give you guidance on

- what books to read

- your practical skills

- how to study and practise

- when you're ready for your tests

- further training after passing your practical test.

It isn't necessary for someone to be on the ADI register to give training for the theory test alone. You may find a training course to help you to prepare for the test. Look in your local paper or visit your local library for information.

There are also videos and CD-ROMs available to help you to study. The CD-ROM *Driving Skills: The Theory Test and Beyond* helps you to learn interactively and goes beyond the theory test, teaching you driving skills for life. There are also mock theory test papers that have been produced by various companies. Visit your local bookshop or ask your driving instructor about relevant material.

If you want to ride a motorcycle

Before you take your practical test you must attend and successfully complete a Compulsory Basic Training (CBT) course (except in Northern Ireland). CBT courses can only be given by training bodies approved by DSA. Frequent checks are made to ensure a high standard of instruction.

The course will include

- classroom training

- practical skills training.

You can find out about CBT courses from

- your local Road Safety Officer

- your motorcycle dealer

- DSA Tel: 0115 901 2500.

You'll have to answer specific questions on motorcycling in the theory test. DSA's *The Motorcycling Manual* (The Stationery Office) tells you about motorcycling skills in more detail. Books from other publishers are also available. In addition, buy and read a copy of *The Highway Code*. Keep it and refer to it after you've passed your tests. Make sure that you have the latest copy as it's updated periodically.

Applying for your licence

You'll need to apply for a provisional licence as you must produce it at the theory test centre. An application form (D1) can be obtained from any post office.

When you receive your provisional licence sign it immediately. Don't drive until you've done so.

About the theory test

The actual delivery of the test is undertaken by DriveSafe Services Ltd, although DSA has overall responsibility for managing the theory test operation.

The theory test is straightforward and you'll pass if you're well prepared. You need to have a knowledge of *The Highway Code* and understand the principles of road safety.

Does everyone have to take the theory test?

If you don't hold a full UK or full European Economic Areas (EEA) licence you'll have to take a theory test. If you hold a full licence for another category of vehicle you may not have to take the test. Holders of a full car licence who wish to obtain a motorcycle licence don't have to take the theory test. Nor will holders of a full motorcycle licence who require a full car licence. If you passed a theory test and then a practical

moped test then you won't have to take the theory test again in order to upgrade to a car or motorcycle licence.

Can I take my practical test first?

No. You have to take and pass your theory test before a booking for the practical test is accepted.

Will I be asked to do lots of writing?

No. The question paper is designed so that you only have to put a cross against the answers you think are correct.

How many questions are there?

There are 35 questions in the paper. You should try to answer all of them.

How long do I have to complete the test?

Each test session lasts for 40 minutes. You can take all this time if you need to, and there will be a clock in the room to remind you of the time. The invigilator will also tell you when there's five minutes left.

You'll be asked to surrender any material such as books and papers before the start of the test.

Where do I have to go to take the test?

There are over 150 test centres throughout England, Scotland, Wales and Northern Ireland. Most people have a test centre within 20 miles of their home but this will vary depending on the density of the population. You can find a list of test centres at the back of this book or telephone the information line 0645 000 555.

When are the test centres open?

Sessions are provided on weekdays, evenings and on Saturdays. However, where demand is less than 100 tests per year test sessions may be less frequent.

Will I know the result straight away?

Not straight away, but you'll be informed in about seven to ten days.

Some centres provide a facility for results as you wait. You can ask about details of this service when you book your test.

If I don't pass when can I take the test again?

You will have to wait a minimum of three days before you take the test again. If you fail your test you've shown that you aren't fully prepared. Good preparation will save you time and money.

Is the test only available in English?

No. The paper is available in the following languages

English	Chinese
Gujerati	Welsh
Hindi	Bengali
Punjabi	Urdu

If you can speak English but can't read in the languages provided a member of staff will be available to read through the test on a one-to-one basis. State this on your application form or tell the operator when you call to book your test.

Can I bring a translator with me?

Yes. If you can't read or write any of the languages available you're allowed to bring a translator with you when you take your test. You can only bring a translator who's approved by the DSA as independent. Normally they should be a member of a suitable professional institute, such as the Institute of Translation and Interpreting (ITT) or the Institute of Linguists. You should inform the booking office that you intend to bring a translator with you. They can provide a list of approved organisations

A DriveSafe booking operator

Are there any provisions for special needs?

Every effort has been made to ensure that the theory test can be taken by all candidates. It's important that you tell the operator or state your needs on your application form so that the necessary arrangements can be made.

If you're dyslexic or have difficulty with reading, don't worry. You'll be allowed double the normal time to take the test if it's necessary. Normally you'll have to provide a statement to confirm that extra time is needed. If it isn't possible to obtain a statement from a professional teacher or tutor then DSA will consider a statement from an independent person who knows something about your reading ability. This could be your employer, but if you're unsure about who to ask telephone the theory test information line 0645 000 555 for advice. If you have extreme difficulties a reader can be provided.

If you're deaf and also have difficulty reading, a British Sign Language signer or lip-speaker can be provided. If you have any physical disability that could prevent you marking the boxes on the test paper help will be available for you.

If you require wheelchair access and your nearest test centre doesn't provide this DSA will arrange for you to take the test in your home, or take you to another test centre where the facilities are provided. Telephone the theory test information line for more details.

How do I book a test?

Application forms are available from

- theory test centres
- driving test centres
- your Approved Driving Instructor.

The easiest way to book a test is by telephone, using your credit or debit card. If you book by this method you'll be given the date and time of your test immediately. You can do this by calling 0645 000 666 at any time between 8 am and 6 pm Monday to Friday. When you phone you should have ready your

- DVLA licence number
- credit or debit card details. If you're deaf and need a minicom machine ring 0645 700 301.

Welsh speakers can ring 0645 700 201.

You'll be given a booking number. Take this together with your signed driving licence and photo identity when you attend your theory test.

At the test centre

Make sure that you have all the necessary documents with you. You'll need

- your signed driving licence
- your appointment card or booking number
- photo identity.

The form of photographic identification acceptable at both theory and practical tests are as follows:

- **your passport**. This doesn't have to be a British passport
- **cheque guarantee card or credit card** with a signature and photograph of the candidate
- **an employer's identity or workplace pass** with candidate's photograph and their name or signature or both
- **Trade Union Card** with candidate's photograph and signature
- **Student Union Card** with reference to either the NUS or an education establishment/course reference number. The card must display the candidate's photograph or signature or both
- **School Bus Pass** with the name of the issuing authority and a photograph and signature of the candidate

I _____(name of acceptable person) certify that this is a true likeness of,

_____ (name of candidate), who has been known to me for____(number) months / years in r capacity as_____ (specify capacit

Signed_____

Dated_____

Business or profession (and registration certificate number, if any)_____

Telephone number_____

- **card issued in connection with sale and purchase of reduced price railway tickets** with the name of the issuing authority. This is a card issued by a Railway Authority or other authorised body to purchase a reduced price railway ticket (e.g. a Young Persons Railcard).
- **Gun Licence** this includes a Firearm or Shotgun Certificate which bears the photograph and signature of the candidate
- **Proof of Age Card** issued by the Portman Group with the candidate's photograph and signature
- **A Standard Acknowlegement Letter (SAL)** issued by the Home Office with photograph and signature of the candidate.

No photo
No licence
No test

If you don't have any of these you can bring a photograph, together with a statement that it's a true likeness of you. This can be signed by any of the following

- Approved Driving Instructor
- DSA-certified Motorcycle instructor
- Member of Parliament
- medical practitioner
- local authority councillor
- teacher (qualified)
- Justice of the Peace
- civil servant (established)
- police officer
- bank official
- minister of religion
- barrister or solicitor
- Commissioned Officer in Her Majesty's Forces.

If you don't bring these documents on the day you won't be able to take your test and you'll lose your fee. If you have any queries about what photographic evidence we will accept, contact the enquiry line.

Arrive in plenty of time so that you aren't rushed. The test centre staff will check your documents and ensure that you have the right category test paper to complete. If you arrive after the session has started you will not be allowed to sit the test.

THEORY TEST FOR DRIVERS
PRACTICE QUESTIONS

Surname

First Names

Booking Ref. 🔒🔒

Pro. Licence No.

ENGLISH M.V.

Centre No.

	D	D	M	M	Y	Y	Y	Y

Date

	H	H	M	M

Time

GENERAL INSTRUCTIONS

1. For each question you must find the right answer(s) and mark an X in the box next to it.
2. Do not write any comments on your test paper.
3. Two examples have been done to show you how to mark your answers.
4. If you make a mistake cross out your original choice completely

and mark your other choice as shown.

EXAMPLES

E1 What MUST you have before you are allowed to drive in the UK?

Mark one answer

a ☒ A medical certificate

b ☒ A signed passport photograph

c ☒ A signed driving licence

d ☒ A copy of your birth certificate

E2 Which TWO would help you to have a safe long journey?

Mark two answers

a ☒ Drive through the town centres

b ☒ Use a map to plan your journey

c ☒ Start out in plenty of time

d ☒ Set a time limit for your journey

e ☒ Avoid having breaks until near the end

P1 This sign means

Mark one answer

a ☒ follow the tracks

b ☒ slippery road ahead

c ☒ change lanes

d ☒ vehicles liable to pass

P2 You MUST stop when signalled to do so by which THREE of these?

Mark three answers

a ☒ A police officer

b ☒ A pedestrian

c ☒ A school crossing patrol

d ☒ A bus driver

e ☒ A red traffic light

P3 What should you use the hard shoulder of a motorway for?

Mark one answer

a ☒ Stopping in an emergency

b Overtaking

c ☒ Stopping when you are tired

d ☒ Joining the motorway

P4 What should the driver of the red car do?

Mark one answer

a ☒ Pull out quickly

b ☒ Continue to wait for a safe gap in the traffic

c ☒ Continue to wait until the traffic lights change

d ☒ Gesture to the driver of the white car to ask her to stop

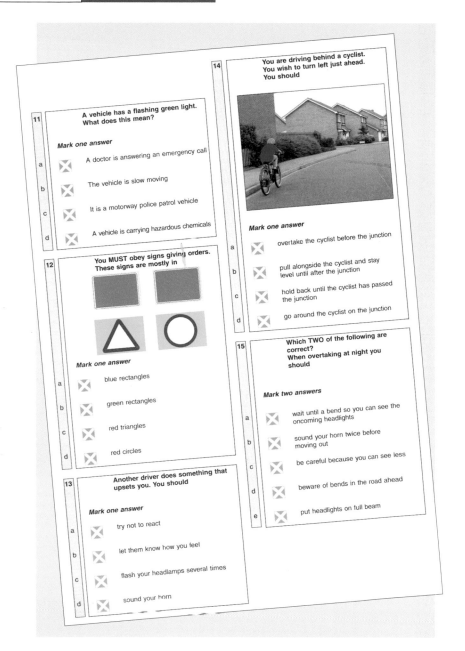

11 A vehicle has a flashing green light. What does this mean?

Mark one answer

a A doctor is answering an emergency call

b The vehicle is slow moving

c It is a motorway police patrol vehicle

d A vehicle is carrying hazardous chemicals

12 You MUST obey signs giving orders. These signs are mostly in

Mark one answer

a blue rectangles

b green rectangles

c red triangles

d red circles

13 Another driver does something that upsets you. You should

Mark one answer

a try not to react

b let them know how you feel

c flash your headlamps several times

d sound your horn

14 You are driving behind a cyclist. You wish to turn left just ahead. You should

Mark one answer

a overtake the cyclist before the junction

b pull alongside the cyclist and stay level until after the junction

c hold back until the cyclist has passed the junction

d go around the cyclist on the junction

15 Which TWO of the following are correct? When overtaking at night you should

Mark two answers

a wait until a bend so you can see the oncoming headlights

b sound your horn twice before moving out

c be careful because you can see less

d beware of bends in the road ahead

e put headlights on full beam

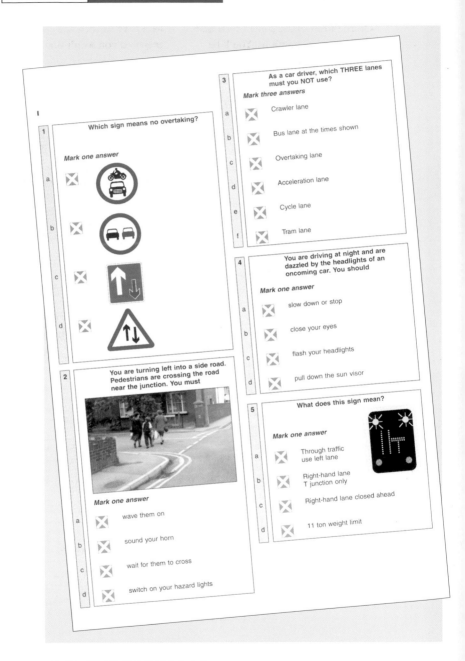

I

1 Which sign means no overtaking?

Mark one answer

a

b

c

d

2 You are turning left into a side road. Pedestrians are crossing the road near the junction. You must

Mark one answer

a wave them on

b sound your horn

c wait for them to cross

d switch on your hazard lights

3 As a car driver, which THREE lanes must you NOT use?

Mark three answers

a Crawler lane

b Bus lane at the times shown

c Overtaking lane

d Acceleration lane

e Cycle lane

f Tram lane

4 You are driving at night and are dazzled by the headlights of an oncoming car. You should

Mark one answer

a slow down or stop

b close your eyes

c flash your headlights

d pull down the sun visor

5 What does this sign mean?

Mark one answer

a Through traffic use left lane

b Right-hand lane T junction only

c Right-hand lane closed ahead

d 11 ton weight limit

On the front of the paper you'll find some practice questions. You'll be given time to look at and attempt these before the test begins.

There will be different types of questions in the paper. Most of them will ask you to mark ONE correct answer from four. Other questions will ask for TWO or more correct answers from a selection. Some of the questions will show you a picture. This is to test your knowledge of traffic signs or your ability to spot a hazard. Look at it carefully.

The questions will cover a variety of topics relating to road safety. Mark the box alongside the answers you think are correct.

Some questions will take longer to answer than others. The questions won't try to trick you. If you're well prepared you won't find them difficult. Take your time and read the questions carefully. You're given plenty of time, so relax and don't rush. Attempt to answer all 35 questions.

If you have learning difficulties, don't worry – you'll be given extra time to complete your question paper.

When you think you've finished look at the paper again and check your answers before you hand the paper in.

If you're taking a motorcycle theory test

As well as questions that apply to all road users, you'll be asked some specific questions on motorcycling matters.

The topics covered in the question paper

ALERTNESS

The need to be alert and attentive when driving or riding. You must consider

- **Observation**   looking all around for other road users and pedestrians.

- **Anticipation**   looking ahead and giving yourself enough time to react to hazards.

- **Concentration**   being alert at all times when driving or riding.

- **Awareness**   understanding the actions of other road users.

- **Distraction**   not becoming distracted whilst driving or riding. Your attention must be on the road

ATTITUDE

Your attitude will affect your driving. Attitude consists of

- **Consideration**   considering other road users. Be positive but treat them as you would wish to be treated.

- **Positioning**   not following too closely. As well as being dangerous, it can feel threatening to the driver in front.

- **Courtesy**   treating other road users as colleagues or team members. They too are trying to complete their journey safely.

- **Priority**   being aware that all rules on priority won't always be followed by other road users. Try to be calm and tolerant if other drivers or riders break the rules.

SAFETY AND YOUR VEHICLE

To prevent your vehicle endangering lives you must ensure that it's in good condition. You should be aware of

- **Fault detection**   being able to detect minor faults on your vehicle.

- **Defects**   an unroadworthy vehicle which might endanger your passengers or other road users.

- **Safety equipment**   if you need to use safety equipment you should know the correct way to use it.

- **Emissions**   your vehicle must comply with correct emissions regulations.

- **Noise**   vehicles are noisy. Prevent excessive noise, especially at night.

SAFETY MARGINS

You must be aware of the safety margins when driving in all conditions.
You should consider

- **Stopping distances**   leaving enough room to stop in all conditions.

- **Road surfaces**   being aware of uneven or slippery surfaces.

- **Skidding**   preventing a skid is most important, but you should also be aware of how to react in the event of you losing control of your vehicle.

- **Weather conditions**   realising that weather conditions will have an effect on how your vehicle behaves.

HAZARD AWARENESS

Your good judgement and perception of the road ahead will lessen the risk of an accident. You should keep in mind

- **Anticipation**   planning ahead to prevent last-second reactions.

- **Hazard awareness**   recognising a hazard ahead and preparing yourself for it.

- **Attention**   looking out for problems ahead when you're driving or riding.

- **Speed and distance**   travelling at the correct speed for the situation. Leave enough distance to react if a problem arises.

- **Reaction time**   being aware that you need time to react.

- **Alcohol and drugs**   these will affect your reaction time.

- **Tiredness**   don't drive or ride if you're tired. You need to be aware at all times.

VULNERABLE ROAD USERS

Others on the road may need more time or room. Potential hazards to consider are

- **Pedestrians**   be aware of their actions as they cross the road.

- **Children**   particularly unpredictable on and around roads.

- **People with disabilities**   might not be able to react to danger as quickly or easily as the able-bodied.

- **Motorcyclists**   be aware of their presence on the road.

- **Cyclists**   may need to swerve to avoid obstructions or poor road surfaces, and are often affected by weather conditions.

- **Horse riders**   animals can be unpredictable and may move rather slowly.

OTHER TYPES OF VEHICLE

Other vehicles might behave differently on the road. You should consider

- **Motorcycles**   need as much room as a car.

- **Lorries**   are larger and need more room on the road.

- **Buses**   are usually large and might make frequent stops.

VEHICLE HANDLING

You need to adapt your driving or riding to the different conditions on the road. You should be aware of

- **Weather conditions**   wet or icy roads will affect the handling of your vehicle.

- **Road conditions**   the road surface may affect your vehicle.

- **Time of day**   hazards when driving or riding at night.

- **Speed**   it's more difficult to control your vehicle at high speeds.

- **Traffic calming**   measures to slow down traffic where there are pedestrians.

MOTORWAY RULES

You must know the rules that apply to you and your vehicle on the motorway. Factors to consider are

- **Speed limits**   being aware of the speed restrictions on the motorway.

- **Lane discipline** keeping to the left unless overtaking.

- **Stopping**   knowing when and where you can stop on the motorway.

- **Lighting**   being aware of the importance of being seen.

- **Parking**   not parking on the motorway unless in an emergency.

RULES OF THE ROAD

You should know the rules of the road. Aspects include

- **Speed limits**   being aware of the speed limits for different types of vehicle.

- **Parking**   choosing a sensible place to park.

- **Lighting**   not letting your vehicle become a hazard.

ROAD AND TRAFFIC SIGNS

Traffic signs are a means of giving messages to road users. You should know what they mean. You should consider

- **Road signs**   they tell you about the road ahead.

- **Speed limits**   recognise signs showing speed limits.

- **Road markings** directions might be painted on the road surface.

- **Regulations**   these can be shown to you by means of a road sign.

DOCUMENTS

You and your vehicle must be licenced to be on the road. The documents you'll need include

- **Licence**   you must know what the law requires.

- **Insurance**   you must have the cover you need to drive or ride.

- **MOT**   you should be aware of the safety checks your vehicle must
  certificate   undergo to gain an MOT certificate.

ACCIDENTS

You should know what to do if you arrive at or are involved in an accident.
You should be aware of

- **First Aid**   if you're qualified and fit, your fast, effective action
              might save a life.

- **Warning**   knowing how to warn other road users of an accident.
  devices

- **Reporting**   knowing where and when to report an accident.
  procedures

- **Safety**   knowing what to do if a vehicle carrying hazardous
  regulations   loads is involved in an accident.

VEHICLE LOADING

You should be aware of the the importance of secure loads. You should consider

- **Stability**   making sure that your load doesn't affect the stability of
              your vehicle.

- **Towing**   being aware of the effects of towing a trailer and the rules
              that apply.

About Part Three

In this part of the book you'll find questions that might be used in your theory test. The answers have been provided to help you to study.

For easy reference and to help you to study, the questions have been divided into topics and put into sections. Although this isn't how you'll find them on your question paper it's helpful if you want to refer to particular subjects.

In Part Three the questions are in the left-hand column with a choice of answers beneath. On the right-hand side of the page you'll find the correct answers and a brief explanation of why the answers are correct. There will also be some advice on correct driving procedures.

DON'T JUST LEARN THE ANSWERS. It's important that you know **why** the answers are correct. This will help you with your practical skills and prepare you to become a safe and confident driver. Taking exams or tests is rarely a pleasant experience but you can make it easier by being confident that you have the knowledge to answer the questions correctly.

Make studying more fun by involving friends and relations. Take part in a question-and-answer game. Test those 'experienced' drivers who've had their licence a while: they might learn something too!

If you're taking a motorcycle theory test

In this part of the book the specific questions for motorcyclists are marked with a motorcycle symbol.

Most of the other questions refer to all road users, so you should study these too. Some will appear on your paper with slight changes, for example 'rider' instead of 'driver' or 'headlight' instead of 'headlights'.

SECTION 1 ALERTNESS

This section looks at alertness and attention when you're driving.

The questions will ask you about

- observation

- anticipation

- concentration

- awareness

- distraction

- boredom.

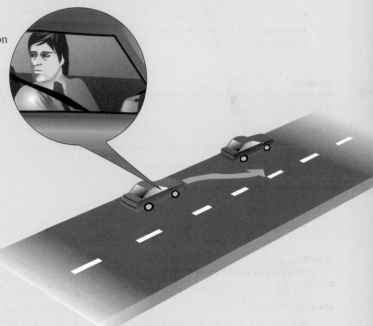

Question
When turning your car in the road you should

Mark one answer

☒ overhang the kerb

☒ use a driveway if possible

☒ check all around for other road users

☒ keep your hand on the handbrake throughout.

Answer

☒ check all around for other road users

There might be an occasion when you need to turn your car around to face the opposite way. Ensure that you're fully aware of other road users by practising good observation. The road you intend to turn around in shouldn't be busy. If it is, find a quiet side road to turn in.

Question
Before you make a U-turn, in the road you should

Mark one answer

☒ look over your shoulder for a final check

☒ signal so that other drivers can slow down for you

☒ give arm signals as well as use your indicators

☒ select a higher gear than normal.

Answer

☒ look over your shoulder for a final check

If you want to make a U-turn, slow down and ensure that the road is clear in both directions. Make sure that the road is wide enough to carry out the manoeuvre safely.

Question
To move off safely from a parked position you should

Mark one answer

☒ signal if other drivers will need to slow down

☒ NOT look round if there is a parked vehicle close in front of you

☒ give a hand signal as well as using your indicators

☒ use your mirrors and look round for a final check.

Answer

☒ use your mirrors and look round for a final check

When moving off from the side of the road you should always use your mirrors. Look all around for a final check. There may be a road user you haven't seen in your mirrors.

Question

To move off safely from a parked position you should

Mark one answer

☒ signal if other drivers will need to slow down

☒ NOT look round if there is a parked vehicle close in front of you

☒ give a hand signal as well as using your indicators

☒ look over your shoulder for a final check.

Answer

look over your shoulder for a final check

If you're intending to move off from the side of the road on a motorcycle you must take a final look around over your shoulder. There may be another road user not visible in your mirrors.

Question

What, according to *The Highway Code*, do the letters MSM mean?

Mark one answer

☒ Mirror, signal, manoeuvre.

☒ Manoeuvre, signal, mirror.

☒ Mirror, speed, manoeuvre.

☒ Manoeuvre, speed, mirror.

Answer

Mirror, signal, manoeuvre.

Always use this routine when you're approaching a hazard.

Use your mirrors to check the position of traffic around you. Signal your intention to change course or slow down. Do this in good time. A 'manoeuvre' is any change of speed or position, from slowing or stopping the car to turning off a busy main road.

Question

When riding, you find your shoulders obstruct your mirrors. To overcome this you should

Mark one answer

☒ extend the mirror arms

☒ fit smaller mirrors

☒ use your indicators earlier than normal

☒ not use the mirrors.

Answer

extend the mirror arms

It's essential that you have a clear view all around. Check the position of the mirrors before you move off.

Question
You are just about to turn right. What should you do just before you turn?

Mark one answer

☒ Give the correct signal.

☒ Take a 'lifesaver' glance over your shoulder.

☒ Select the correct gear.

☒ Get in position ready for the turn.

Answer

☒ **Take a 'lifesaver' glance over your shoulder.**

When you're turning right plan your approach to the junction. Signal and select the correct gear in good time. Just before you turn give a 'lifesaver' glance to the rear for a final check behind and alongside.

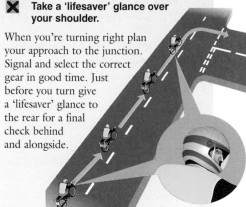

Question
What is the 'lifesaver' when riding a motorcycle?

Mark one answer

☒ A certificate every motorcyclist MUST have.

☒ A final, rearward glance before changing direction.

☒ A part of the motorcycle tool kit.

☒ A mirror fitted to check blind spots.

Answer

☒ **A final, rearward glance before changing direction.**

This action makes you aware of what's happening behind and alongside. This glance should be timed so that you still have time to react if it isn't safe to perform the manoeuvre.

Question
What is the safest way to brake?

Mark one answer

☒ Brake lightly, then harder as you begin to stop, then ease off just before stopping.

☒ Brake hard, put your gear lever into neutral and pull your handbrake on just before stopping.

☒ Brake lightly, push your clutch pedal down and pull your handbrake on just before stopping.

☒ Put your gear lever into neutral, brake hard, then ease off just before stopping.

Answer

☒ **Brake lightly, then harder as you begin to stop, then ease off just before stopping.**

Try to plan ahead so you don't need to brake harshly. Brake lightly, then harder as you begin to stop, then ease off just before stopping. Don't put your gear lever into neutral until you come to a complete stop, as this might cause a loss of control.

Question

You are driving on a wet road. You have to stop your vehicle in an emergency. You should

Mark one answer

☒ apply the handbrake and footbrake together

☒ keep both hands on the wheel

☒ select reverse gear

☒ give an arm signal.

Answer

☒ **keep both hands on the wheel**

As you drive look well ahead and all around so that you're ready for any hazards that might occur. There may be occasions when you have to stop in an emergency. React as soon as you can whilst keeping control of the vehicle.

Question

You see road signs showing a sharp bend ahead. What should you do?

Mark one answer

☒ Continue at the same speed.

☒ Slow down as you go around the bend.

☒ Slow down as you come out of the bend.

☒ Slow down before the bend.

Answer

☒ **Slow down before the bend.**

Road signs might give you warning of a hazard ahead. Always look and plan well ahead. This will avoid the need for late, harsh braking. Your motorcycle should be upright and moving in a straight line when you brake. This will ensure maximum control when dealing with the hazard.

Question

As you approach this bridge you should

Mark three answers

☒ move into the middle of the road to get a better view

☒ slow down

☒ get over the bridge as quickly as possible

☒ consider using your horn

☒ find another route

☒ beware of pedestrians.

Answers

☒ **slow down**

☒ **consider using your horn**

☒ **beware of pedestrians**

Consider the hidden hazards and be ready to react if necessary.

Question

You are taking drugs that are likely to affect your driving. What should you do?

Mark one answer

☒ Seek medical advice before driving.

☒ Limit your driving to essential journeys.

☒ Only drive if accompanied by a full licence-holder.

☒ Drive only for short distances.

Answer

☒ **Seek medical advice before driving.**

Check with your doctor or pharmacist if you think that the drugs you're taking are likely to make you feel drowsy.

Question

If you are feeling tired it is best to stop as soon as you can. Until then you should

Mark one answer

☒ increase your speed to find a stopping place quickly

☒ ensure a supply of fresh air

☒ gently tap the steering wheel

☒ keep changing speed to improve concentration.

Answer

☒ **ensure a supply of fresh air**

If you're travelling on a long journey plan your route before you leave. This will help you to

- be decisive at intersections and junctions
- plan your rest stops
- know approximately how long the journey will take.

Make sure that the vehicle you're travelling in is well ventilated. A warm, stuffy atmosphere can make you drowsy, which will impair your judgement and perception.

Question

Your reactions will be much slower when driving

Mark one answer

☒ if tired

☒ in fog

☒ too quickly

☒ in rain.

Answer

☒ **if tired**

Try to prevent becoming tired by

- taking plenty of rest stops
- allowing fresh air into the vehicle.

Question

You are driving on a motorway. You feel tired. You should

Mark one answer

☒ carry on but drive slowly

☒ leave the motorway at the next exit

☒ complete your journey as quickly as possible

☒ stop on the hard shoulder.

Question

You are planning to drive a long distance. Which THREE things will make the journey safer?

Mark three answers

☒ Avoid travelling at night.

☒ Ensure a supply of fresh air.

☒ Avoid motorways.

☒ Make stops for refreshments.

☒ Drive slowly.

Question

How often should you stop on a long journey?

Mark one answer

☒ When you need petrol.

☒ At least every four hours.

☒ At least every two hours.

☒ When you need to eat.

Answer

☒ **leave the motorway at the next exit**

If you do feel tired and there's no service station for many miles, leave the motorway at the next exit. Find a road off the motorway where you can pull up and stop.

Answers

☒ **Avoid travelling at night.**

☒ **Ensure a fresh supply of air.**

☒ **Make stops for refreshment.**

If you're travelling a long distance plan your journey carefully. Ensure you plan rest stops too so that you don't become tired. This will also help to prevent any passengers becoming restless and possibly distracting you.

Answer

☒ **At least every two hours.**

Your judgement and perception will be affected if you aren't alert. Tiredness could endanger your passengers and other road users as well as yourself.

Question

Which TWO things would help to keep you alert during a long journey?

Mark two answers

- ☒ Finish your journey as fast as you can.
- ☒ Keep off the motorways and use country roads.
- ☒ Make sure that you get plenty of fresh air.
- ☒ Make regular stops for refreshments.

Answers

- ✖ **Make sure that you get plenty of fresh air.**
- ✖ **Make regular stops for refreshments.**

Make sure that the vehicle you're driving is well ventilated. A warm, stuffy atmosphere will make you feel drowsy. Open a window or turn down the heating.

Question

Which THREE are likely to make you lose concentration while driving?

Mark three answers

- ☒ Looking at road maps.
- ☒ Listening to loud music.
- ☒ Using your windscreen washers.
- ☒ Looking in your wing mirror.
- ☒ Using a mobile phone.

Answers

- ✖ **Looking at road maps.**
- ✖ **Listening to loud music.**
- ✖ **Using a mobile phone.**

Looking at road maps while driving is very dangerous. If you aren't sure of your route stop in a safe place and check the map. You must not allow anything to take your attention away from the road.

If you wish to use a mobile phone, stop in a safe place before doing so. If you use a mobile phone frequently have a 'hands free' phone fitted in your vehicle.

Question

You have not worn suitable riding gear and get cold and wet when riding. Which TWO are likely effects?

Mark two answers

- ☒ You may lose concentration.
- ☒ Your visor may freeze up.
- ☒ You may slide off the seat.
- ☒ Your reaction times may slow.
- ☒ Your helmet may loosen.

Answers

- ✖ **You may lose concentration.**
- ✖ **Your reaction times may slow.**

If you're riding a motorcycle you should ensure that you're wearing suitable clothing. If you become cold and uncomfortable this could cause you to lose concentration.

Question

A driver pulls out of a side road in front of you. You have to brake hard. You should

Mark one answer

☒ ignore the error and stay calm

☒ flash your lights to show your annoyance

☒ sound your horn to show your annoyance

☒ overtake as soon as possible.

Answer

☒ **ignore the error and stay calm**

If you're driving or riding where there are a number of side roads, be alert. Drivers approaching or emerging from the side road might not be able to see you. Be especially careful if there are a lot of parked vehicles. If a vehicle does emerge and you have to stop quickly

- try to be tolerant
- learn from the experience.

Question

A car driver pulls out causing you to brake. You should

Mark one answer

☒ keep calm and not retaliate

☒ overtake and sound your horn

☒ drive close behind and sound your horn

☒ flag the driver down and explain the mistake.

Answer

☒ **keep calm and not retaliate**

You have to understand that others on the road might disobey the rules or make an error of judgement at times. Try to accept this calmly and learn from other people's mistakes.

Question

Another driver does something that upsets you. You should

Mark one answer

☒ try not to react

☒ let them know how you feel

☒ flash your headlamps several times

☒ sound your horn.

Answer

☒ **try not to react**

There are occasions when other drivers or riders make a misjudgement or a mistake. If this happens try not to let it worry you. Don't react by showing anger. Sounding the horn, flashing the headlamps or shouting at the other driver won't help the situation. Good anticipation will help to prevent these incidents becoming accidents.

Question

Another driver's behaviour has upset you. It may help if you

Mark one answer

☒ stop and take a break

☒ shout abusive language

☒ gesture to them with your hand

☒ follow their car, flashing the headlights.

Answer

☒ **stop and take a break**

Tiredness may make you more irritable than you would be normally. You might react differently to situations because of it. If you feel yourself becoming tense, take a break.

SECTION 6   VULNERABLE ROAD USERS

This section looks at the risks when dealing with vulnerable road users.

The questions will ask you about

- pedestrians
- children
- elderly drivers
- disabled people
- cyclists
- motorcyclists
- animals
- new drivers.

Question

You should not ride too closely behind a lorry because

Mark one answer

☒ you will breathe in the lorry's exhaust fumes

☒ wind from the lorry will slow you down

☒ drivers behind you may not be able to see you

☒ it will reduce your view ahead.

Answer

☒ it will reduce your view ahead

If you're following a large vehicle your view beyond it will be restricted. Drop back. This will help you to see more of the road ahead.

Question

You are riding in fast-flowing traffic. The vehicle behind is following too closely. You should

Mark one answer

☒ slow down gradually to increase the gap in front of you

☒ slow down as quickly as possible by braking

☒ accelerate to get away from the vehicle behind you

☒ apply the brakes briefly to warn the driver behind.

Answer

☒ slow down gradually to increase the gap in front of you

Vehicles travelling too close together is a dangerous practice. Increase the safety margin by dropping back.

Question

You are riding along a main road with many side roads. Why should you be particularly careful?

Mark one answer

☒ Gusts of wind from the side roads may push you off course.

☒ Drivers coming out from side roads may not see you.

☒ The road will be more slippery where cars have been turning.

☒ Drivers will be travelling slowly when they approach a junction.

Answer

☒ Drivers coming out from side roads may not see you.

If you're riding along a main road where there are many side roads be alert. Drivers approaching or emerging from side roads may not be able to see you. Be especially careful if there are a lot of parked vehicles.

Parked car

Always drive at a speed that will enable you to slow down and stop in good time. If you look well ahead and anticipate the actions of other road users you'll avoid having to brake suddenly or harshly.

Question

You are driving on a country road. What should you expect to see coming towards you on YOUR side of the road?

Mark one answer

☒ Motorcycles.

☒ Bicycles.

☒ Horse riders.

☒ Pedestrians.

Answer

☒ **Pedestrians.**

On a quiet country road always be aware that there may be a hazard just around the next bend, such as a slow-moving vehicle or pedestrians. There might not be a pavement and people may be walking on your side of the road.

Question

Which sign means that there may be people walking along the road?

Mark one answer

☒

☒

☒

☒

Answer

☒

Always check the road signs as you drive. They'll keep you informed of hazards ahead and help you to anticipate any problems.

There are different types of signs showing pedestrians. Learn the meaning of each one. This will help you to be aware of the hazard ahead.

Question

What does this sign mean?

Mark one answer

☒ Pedestrian crossing.

☒ Pedestrians in the road ahead.

☒ No pedestrians.

☒ Route for pedestrians.

Answer

☒ **No pedestrians.**

Always be aware that, although the sign restricts pedestrians, there may be some about.

Question

You are turning left into a side road. Pedestrians are crossing the road near the junction. You must

Mark one answer

 wave them on

 sound your horn

 switch on your hazard lights

 wait for them to cross.

Answer

✗ wait for them to cross

Before you turn into a junction check that it's clear. Check the pavement in each direction. If there are pedestrians crossing let them cross in their own time.

Question

You are turning left at a junction. Pedestrians have started to cross the road. You should

Mark one answer

 go on, giving them plenty of room

 stop and wave at them to cross

 blow your horn and proceed

 give way to them.

Answer

✗ give way to them

If you're turning into a side road you should give way to pedestrians already crossing. They have priority. Don't

• wave them across the road

• sound your horn

• flash your lights

• give any other misleading signal – other road users may misinterpret your signal and you might lead the pedestrian into a dangerous situation.

If a pedestrian's slow or indecisive be patient and wait. Don't hurry them across by revving the engine.

Question

You are turning left from a main road into a side road. People are already crossing the road into which you're turning. You should

Mark one answer

- ☒ continue, as it is your right of way
- ☒ signal to them to continue crossing
- ☒ wait and allow them to cross
- ☒ sound your horn to warn them of your presence.

Answer

☒ **wait and allow them to cross**

Always check the road you're turning into. Approaching at the correct speed will allow you enough time to observe and react.

Question

You are at a road junction, turning into a minor road. There are pedestrians crossing the minor road. You should

Mark one answer

- ☒ stop and wave the pedestrians across
- ☒ sound your horn to let the pedestrians know that you are there
- ☒ give way to the pedestrians who are already crossing
- ☒ carry on; the pedestrians should give way to you.

Answer

 give way to the pedestrians who are already crossing

Always look into the road you're turning into. If there are pedestrians crossing, be considerate but don't wave or signal at them to cross. Signal your intention to turn as you approach.

Question

You want to reverse into a side road. You are not sure that the area behind your car is clear. What should you do?

Mark one answer

☒ Look through the rear window only.

☒ Get out and check.

☒ Check the mirrors only.

☒ Carry on, assuming it's clear.

Answer

☒ **Get out and check.**

It's always safer to be sure. You may not be able to see a small child close behind your car. The shape and size of your vehicle can restrict visibility.

Question

You are about to reverse into a side road. A pedestrian wishes to cross behind you. You should

Mark one answer

☒ wave to the pedestrian to stop

☒ give way to the pedestrian

☒ wave to the pedestrian to cross

☒ reverse before the pedestrian starts to cross.

Answer

☒ **give way to the pedestrian**

If you need to reverse into a side road try to find a place that's free from traffic and pedestrians.

Look all around before and during the manoeuvre. Always stop and give way to any pedestrians that wish to cross behind you. Don't

• wave them across the road

• sound the horn

• flash your lights

• give any other misleading signal – other road users may not have seen your signal and you might lead the pedestrian into a dangerous situation.

Question

You are reversing from a driveway and cannot see clearly. There are many pedestrians around. You should

Mark one answer

☒ continue whilst sounding your horn

☒ continue with your hazard lights on

☒ get someone to guide you

☒ continue: it is your right of way.

Answer

☒ **get someone to guide you**

If you can't see clearly it's safer to get help from someone outside the vehicle. They'll be in a better position to see all around the vehicle and along the pavement.

Question

You want to turn right from a junction but your view is restricted by parked vehicles. What should you do?

Mark one answer

- [X] Move out quickly, but be prepared to stop.
- [X] Sound your horn and pull out if there is no reply.
- [X] Stop, then move slowly forward until you have a clear view.
- [X] Stop, get out and look along the main road to check.

Answer

- [X] **Stop, then move slowly forward until you have a clear view.**

If you want to turn right from a junction and your view's restricted STOP. Ease forward until you can see – there might be something approaching.

IF YOU DON'T KNOW, DON'T GO.

Question

In which THREE places would parking your vehicle cause danger or obstruction to other road users?

Mark three answers

- [X] In front of a property entrance.
- [X] At or near a bus stop.
- [X] On your driveway.
- [X] In a marked parking space.
- [X] On the approach to a level crossing.

Answers

- [X] **In front of a property entrance.**
- [X] **At or near a bus stop.**
- [X] **On the approach to a level crossing.**

Don't park your vehicle where parking restrictions apply. Think carefully before you slow down and stop. Look at road markings and signs to ensure that you aren't parking illegally.

Question

What must a driver do at a pelican crossing when the amber light is flashing?

Mark one answer

- [X] Signal the pedestrian to cross.
- [X] Always wait for the green light before proceeding.
- [X] Give way to any pedestrians on the crossing.
- [X] Wait for the red–and–amber light before proceeding.

Answers

- [X] **Give way to any pedestrians on the crossing.**

The amber light allows pedestrians already on the crossing to get to the other side before a green light shows to the traffic. Let them to do this at their own pace.

Question
The approach to a zebra crossing is marked with zigzag lines. Which TWO must you NOT do within the marked area?

Mark two answers

☒ Overtake.

☒ Cross the lines.

☒ Drive at more than 10 mph.

☒ Park.

Answers

☒ **Overtake.**

☒ **Park.**

Parking here will

- block the view for pedestrians wishing to cross the road

- restrict a driver's or rider's view of the crossing.

When you're approaching a pedestrian crossing don't overtake. The pedestrians waiting to cross the road might not see you as you pull alongside the leading vehicle.

Only stop on a pedestrian crossing if it's to avoid an accident. The crossing should be accessible for pedestrians at all times.

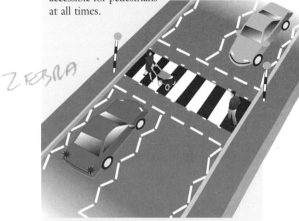

Question
At toucan crossings

Mark two answers

☒ there is no flashing amber light

☒ cyclists are not permitted

☒ there is a continuously flashing amber beacon

☒ pedestrians and cyclists may cross

☒ you only stop if someone is waiting to cross.

Answers

☒ **there is no flashing amber light**

☒ **pedestrians and cyclists may cross**

There are some crossings where cycle routes lead the cyclists to cross at the same place as pedestrians. Always look out for cyclists, as they're likely to be approaching faster than pedestrians.

Question
What type of crossing is this?

Mark one answer

☒ A zebra crossing.

☒ A pelican crossing.

☒ A puffin crossing.

☒ A toucan crossing.

Answer

✖ **A toucan crossing.**

This crossing is similar to a pelican crossing. Cyclists share the crossing with pedestrians without the need to dismount. Watch out for cyclists as they will approach the crossing faster than pedestrians.

Question
When may you stop on a pedestrian crossing?

Mark one answer

☒ Not at any time.

☒ To avoid an accident.

☒ When there's a queue of traffic in front of you.

☒ Between the hours of 11 pm and 7 am.

Answer

✖ **To avoid an accident.**

Don't stop directly on a pedestrian crossing. If you're moving in a queue look well ahead and try to judge the flow of traffic. Leave a gap for pedestrians to cross.

Question
Look at this picture. What is the danger you should be most aware of?

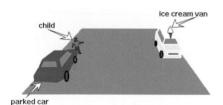

Mark one answer

☒ The ice cream van may move off.

☒ The driver of the ice cream van may get out.

☒ The car on the left may move off.

☒ The child may run out into the road.

Answer

✖ **The child may run out into the road.**

Extra care must be taken when there are children about. Look out for them at all times but especially

• in residential areas

• near parks

• near schools.

Where there are crossing places used by children be extra cautious. Don't

• overtake

• drive at high speed.

If you see an ice cream van ask yourself, 'Where are the children?' They might run across the road to it. Their small size may prevent you seeing them emerging from behind parked vehicles.

Question

You are driving past parked cars. You notice a wheel of a bicycle sticking out between them. What should you do?

Mark one answer

 Accelerate past quickly and sound your horn.

 Slow down and wave the cyclist across.

 Brake sharply and flash your headlights.

 Slow down and be prepared to stop for a cyclist.

Answer

 Slow down and be prepared to stop for a cyclist.

Scan the road as you drive. Try to anticipate hazards by being aware of the likely places where they occur. You'll then be able to react in good time, if necessary.

Question

You are driving past a line of parked cars. You notice a ball bouncing out into the road ahead. What should you do?

Mark one answer

Continue driving at the same speed and sound your horn.

Continue driving at the same speed and flash your headlights.

Slow down and be prepared to stop for children.

Stop and wave the children across to fetch their ball.

Answer

 Slow down and be prepared to stop for children.

Beware of children playing in the street and running out into the road. If a ball bounces out from the pavement slow down and stop. Don't encourage anyone to retrieve it. Other road users may not see your signal and you might lead a child into a dangerous situation.

Question
What does this sign tell you?

Mark one answer

No cycling.

Cycle route ahead.

Route for cycles only.

End of cycle route.

Answer

✖ **Cycle route ahead.**

With people's concern today for the environment, cycle routes are being created in our towns and cities. These can be defined by road markings and signs. Don't straddle or drive in them. Respect the presence of cyclists on the road and give them plenty of room if you need to pass.

Question
What does this sign warn you to look for?

Mark one answer

A school crossing patrol.

A pedestrian crossing.

A park.

School children.

Answer

✖ **School children.**

Look out for road signs as you drive. There could be a sign to warn you that children may be about. If you're driving near a school take extra care, as children can be impulsive and might dart out into the road without warning. Drive at an appropriate speed and try to anticipate their actions.

Question
How will a school crossing patrol signal you to stop?

Mark one answer

By pointing to children on the opposite pavement.

By displaying a red light.

By displaying a stop sign.

By giving you an arm signal.

Answer

✖ **By displaying a stop sign.**

If someone steps out into the road with a school crossing sign you must stop. Don't

• wave anyone across the road

• get impatient or rev your engine.

Question
You see someone step into the road holding this sign. What must you do?

Mark one answer
- ☒ Slow down and look out for children.
- ☒ Signal the person to cross.
- ☒ Drive carefully round the person.
- ☒ Pull up before the person.

Question
A school crossing patrol shows this sign. What must you do?

Mark one answer
- ☒ Continue if it is safe to do so.
- ☒ Slow down and be ready to stop.
- ☒ Stop ONLY if children are crossing.
- ☒ Stop at all times.

Answer
☒ **Pull up before the person.**

Check the road signs as you drive. If you see a sign for a school there might be a school crossing patrol ahead, especially if amber flashing lights show beneath it.

Answer
☒ **Stop at all times.**

Question

You are approaching a school crossing patrol. When this sign is held up you must

Mark one answer

- ☒ stop and allow any children to cross
- ☒ stop and beckon the children to cross
- ☒ stop only if the children are on a pedestrian crossing
- ☒ stop only when the children are actually crossing the road.

Answer

☒ **stop and allow any children to cross**

If you see a school sign anticipate that there might be a school crossing patrol. Always drive carefully where there might be children.

Question

Where would you see this sign?

Mark one answer

- ☒ In the window of a car taking children to school.
- ☒ At the side of the road.
- ☒ At playground areas.
- ☒ On the rear of a school bus or coach.

Answer

☒ **On the rear of a school bus or coach.**

Vehicles that are used to carry children to and from school will be travelling at busy times of the day. If you're following a vehicle with this sign be prepared for it to make frequent stops. It might pick up or set down passengers in places other than normal bus stops.

Question

Where would you see this sign?

Mark one answer

- ☒ On the approach to a school crossing.
- ☒ At a playground entrance.
- ☒ On a school bus.
- ☒ At a 'pedestrians only' area.

Answer

☒ **On a school bus.**

Watch out for children crossing the road from the other side of the bus.

DSA THEORY TEST for car drivers and motorcyclists

Question

You are parking your vehicle in the street. The car parked in front of you is displaying an orange badge. You should

Mark one answer

☒ park close to it to save road space

☒ allow room for a wheelchair

☒ wait until the orange-badge holder returns

☒ park with two wheels on the pavement.

Answer

☒ allow room for a wheelchair

Think about the room that's needed to open the rear of the vehicle and lift a chair in. Room might be needed to manoeuvre a chair between the two cars.

Question

You are following a car driven by an elderly driver. You should

Mark one answer

☒ expect the driver to drive badly

☒ flash your lights and overtake

☒ be aware that the driver's reactions may not be as fast as yours

☒ stay close behind and drive carefully.

Answer

☒ be aware that the driver's reactions may not be as fast as yours

You must show consideration to other road users. Their reactions may be slower and they might need more time to deal with a situation. Be tolerant and don't lose patience or show your annoyance.

Question

You see a pedestrian carrying a white stick. This shows that the person is

Mark one answer

☒ disabled

☒ deaf

☒ elderly

☒ blind.

Answer

☒ blind

If you see a pedestrian carrying a white stick it will mean that the person is partially sighted or blind. Make allowances for their hesitation at crossings or junctions.

Question

You see a pedestrian with a white stick and two red reflective bands. This means that the person is

Mark one answer

☒ physically disabled

☒ deaf only

☒ blind only

☒ deaf and blind.

Answer

✖ **deaf and blind**

If the person is deaf as well as blind the stick will have two red reflective bands. You can't tell if a pedestrian is deaf. Don't assume everyone can hear you approaching.

Question

What action would you take when elderly people are crossing the road?

Elderly people

Mark one answer

☒ Wave them across so they know that you've seen them.

☒ Be patient and allow them to cross in their own time.

☒ Rev the engine to let them know that you're waiting.

☒ Tap the horn in case they are hard of hearing.

Answer

✖ **Be patient and allow them to cross in their own time.**

Don't hurry elderly people across the road by driving up close to them or revving the engine. Be aware that they might take longer to cross. They might also be hard of hearing and not able to hear your approach.

Question

You are following a motorcyclist on an uneven road. You should

Mark one answer

☒ allow less room to ensure that you can be seen in their mirrors

☒ overtake immediately

☒ allow extra room in case they swerve to avoid pot-holes

☒ allow the same room as normal because motorcyclists are not affected by road surfaces.

Answer

✖ **allow extra room in case they swerve to avoid pot-holes**

Pot-holes in the road can unsteady a motorcyclist. For this reason the rider might swerve to avoid an uneven road surface. Watch out at places where this is likely to occur.

Question

You are driving behind a cyclist. You wish to turn left just ahead. You should

Mark one answer

- [ ] overtake the cyclist before the junction
- [ ] pull alongside the cyclist and stay level until after the junction
- [ ] hold back until the cyclist has passed the junction
- [ ] go around the cyclist on the junction.

Answer

✗ hold back until the cyclist has passed the junction

When driving or riding make allowances for cyclists. Allow them plenty of room. If you're following a cyclist be aware that they also have to deal with hazards around them. They might swerve or change direction suddenly to avoid an uneven road surface.

Question

You should NEVER attempt to overtake a cyclist

Mark one answer

- [ ] just before you turn left
- [ ] just before you turn right
- [ ] on a one-way street
- [ ] on a dual carriageway.

Answer

✗ just before you turn left

If you want to turn left and there's a cyclist in front of you, hold back. Wait until the cyclist has passed the junction and then turn left behind them.

Question

You are coming up to a roundabout. A cyclist is signalling to turn right. What should you do?

Mark one answer

- [ ] Overtake on the right.
- [ ] Give a horn warning.
- [ ] Signal the cyclist to move across.
- [ ] Give the cyclist plenty of room.

Answer

✗ Give the cyclist plenty of room.

If you're following a cyclist who's signalling to turn right at a roundabout leave plenty of room. Give them space and time to get into the correct lane.

Question

You are driving behind two cyclists. They approach a roundabout in the left-hand lane. In which direction should you expect the cyclists to go?

Mark one answer

☒ Left.

☒ Right.

☒ Any direction.

☒ Straight ahead.

Question

You are approaching this roundabout and see the cyclist signal right. Why is the cyclist keeping to the left?

Mark one answer

☒ It is a quicker route for the cyclist.

☒ The cyclist is going to turn left instead.

☒ The cyclist thinks *The Highway Code* does not apply to bicycles.

☒ The cyclist is slower and more vulnerable.

Question

When you are overtaking a cyclist you should leave as much room as you would give to a car. Why is this?

Mark one answer

☒ The cyclist might change lanes.

☒ The cyclist might get off the bike.

☒ The cyclist might swerve.

☒ The cyclist might have to make a right turn.

Answer

☒ Any direction.

If you're following a cyclist into a round-about be aware of them as they might not be taking the exit you anticipate. Cyclists approaching in the left-hand lane may be turning right but may not have been able to get into the correct lane due to the heavy traffic. Give them room.

Answer

☒ The cyclist is slower and more vulnerable.

Cycling in today's heavy traffic can be hazardous. Some cyclists may not feel happy about crossing the path of traffic to take up a position in an outside lane. Be aware of this and understand that, although in the left-hand lane, the cyclist might be turning right.

Answer

☒ The cyclist might swerve.

If you intend to overtake a cyclist look at the road ahead. Check if the cyclist needs to change direction for a parked vehicle or an uneven road surface. When you have a safe place to overtake leave as much room as you would for a car. Don't cut in sharply or pass too closely.

Question
Which TWO should you allow extra room when overtaking?

Mark two answers

☒ Motorcycles.

☒ Tractors.

☒ Bicycles.

☒ Road-sweeping vehicles.

Answers
☒ **Motorcycles.**

☒ **Bicycles.**

Don't pass riders too closely as this may cause them to lose balance. Always leave as much room as you would for a car, and don't cut in.

Question
Why should you allow extra room when overtaking a motorcyclist on a windy day?

Mark one answer

☒ The rider may turn off suddenly to get out of the wind.

☒ The rider may be blown across in front of you.

☒ The rider may stop suddenly.

☒ The rider may be travelling faster than normal.

Answer
☒ **The rider may be blown across in front of you.**

A motorcyclist's position on the road can be affected by high winds. If you're driving or riding on a windy day be aware that the conditions might force a motorcyclist to swerve or wobble. Take this into consideration if you're following or wish to overtake.

Question

Which type of vehicle is most affected by strong winds?

Mark one answer

☒ Tractor.

☒ Motorcycle.

☒ Car.

☒ Tanker.

Answer

 Motorcycle.

Pass a motocyclist leaving plenty of room. Allow space in case the wind blows the motorcyclist across the lane.

Question

You are waiting to come out of a side road. Why should you watch carefully for motorcycles?

Mark one answer

☒ Motorcycles are usually faster than cars.

☒ Police patrols often use motorcycles.

☒ Motorcycles are small and hard to see.

☒ Motorcycles have right of way.

Answer

✗ **Motorcycles are small and hard to see.**

If you're waiting to emerge from a side road watch out for motorcyclists. They're smaller and more difficult to see. Be especially careful if there are parked vehicles restricting your view. There might be a motorcyclist appoaching.

IF YOU DON'T KNOW, DON'T GO.

Question

In daylight, an approaching motorcyclist is using a dipped headlight. Why?

Mark one answer

☒ So that the rider can be seen more easily.

☒ To stop the battery over-charging.

☒ To improve the rider's vision.

☒ The rider is inviting you to proceed.

Answer

✗ **So that the rider can be seen more easily.**

A motorcycle can be lost out of sight behind another vehicle. The use of the headlight helps to make it more conspicuous and therefore more easily seen.

Question

Where should you take **particular** care to look out for motorcyclists and cyclists?

Mark one answer

☒ On dual carriageways.

☒ At junctions.

☒ At zebra crossings.

☒ On one-way streets.

Answer

✗ **At junctions.**

Motorcyclists and cyclists may be more difficult to see on the road. This is especially the case at junctions. You may not be able to see a motorcyclist approaching a junction if your view's blocked by other traffic. Be aware of the possibility. A motorcycle may be travelling as fast as a car, or faster. Make sure that you judge speeds correctly before you emerge.

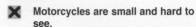

Question
Where **in particular** should you look out for motorcyclists?

Mark one answer

☒ In a filling station.

☒ At a road junction.

☒ Near a service area.

☒ When entering a car park.

Answer

 At a road junction.

Always look ahead and try to make use of the information you see. This will enable you to anticipate possible hazards, and give you more time to deal with them as they occur.

Question
Motorcycle riders are vulnerable because they

Mark one answer

☒ are easy for other road users to see

☒ are difficult for other road users to see

☒ are likely to have breakdowns

☒ cannot give arm signals.

Answer

 are difficult for other road users to see

Motorcyclists don't always wear bright clothing. Look out for and expect to see them at junctions.

Question
Motorcyclists should wear bright clothing mainly because

Mark one answer

☒ they must do so by law

☒ it helps keep them cool in summer

☒ the colours are popular

☒ drivers often do not see them.

Answer

 drivers often do not see them

Although they're advised to wear clothing that's bright or reflective motorcyclists often wear black. This means that they're difficult to see. Look out for them.

Question

Motorcyclists ride in daylight with their headlights switched on because

Mark one answer

☒ it is a legal requirement

☒ there's a speed trap ahead

☒ they need to be seen

☒ there are speed humps ahead.

Answer

☒ **they need to be seen**

Motorcyclists using their headlights in this way aren't indicating any priority. They want you to see them. Riding with the headlight on warns of their approach.

Question

There is a slow-moving motorcyclist ahead of you. You're unsure what the rider is going to do. You should

Mark one answer

☒ pass on the left

☒ pass on the right

☒ stay behind

☒ move closer.

Answer

☒ **stay behind**

Be patient. The motorcyclist might be turning right or changing direction.

Question

You are driving behind a moped. You want to turn left just ahead. You should

Mark one answer

☒ overtake the moped before the junction

☒ pull alongside the moped and stay level until just before the junction

☒ sound your horn as a warning and pull in front of the moped

☒ stay behind until the moped has passed the junction.

Answer

☒ **stay behind until the moped has passed the junction**

Passing the moped and turning into the junction could mean that you cut across the front of the rider. This might force them to slow down, stop or even lose control.

Question

Motorcyclists will often look round over their right shoulder just before turning right. This is because

Mark one answer

☒ they need to listen for following traffic

☒ motorcycles do not have mirrors

☒ looking around helps them balance as they turn

☒ they need to check for traffic in their blind area.

Answer

☒ **they need to check for traffic in their blind area**

If you're behind a motorcyclist who makes a quick glance over their shoulder expect them to be changing direction. They should do this before turning. By observing this you'll get an early signal of their intention.

Question

At road juctions which of the following are most vulnerable?

Mark three answers

[×] Cyclists.

[×] Motorcyclists.

[×] Pedestrians.

[×] Car drivers.

[×] Lorry drivers.

Answers

[×] **Cyclists.**

[×] **Motorcyclists.**

[×] **Pedestrians.**

Good effective observation, coupled with appropriate action, can save lives.

Question

When emerging from a side road into a queue of traffic which vehicles can be especially difficult to see?

Mark one answer

[×] Motorcycles.

[×] Tractors.

[×] Milk floats.

[×] Cars.

Answer

[×] **Motorcycles.**

Your view of the road in both directions can be obscured by parked cars, overgrown hedges or a bend in the road. As you're waiting to emerge don't just expect cars to approach. Look out for other road users too.

Question

You want to turn right from a main road into a side road. Just before turning you should

Mark one answer

[×] cancel your right-turn signal

[×] select first gear

[×] check for traffic overtaking on your right

[×] stop and set the handbrake.

Answer

[×] **check for traffic overtaking on your right**

Motorcyclists often overtake queues of vehicles. Always make that last check in the mirror to avoid turning across their path.

Question

Which of the following are hazards motorcyclists present in queues of traffic?

Mark three answers

- [ ] Cutting in just in front of you.
- [ ] Riding in single file.
- [ ] Passing very close to your car.
- [ ] Riding with their headlamp on dipped beam.
- [ ] Filtering between the lanes.

Answers

- [x] Cutting in just in front of you.
- [x] Passing very close to your car.
- [x] Filtering between the lanes.

Where there's more than one lane of queuing traffic motorcyclists use the opportunity to make progress by riding between the lanes. Be aware that they may be passing on either side. Check your mirrors before you move off.

Question

You are driving on a main road. You intend to turn right into a side road. Just before turning you should

Mark one answer

- [ ] adjust your interior mirror
- [ ] flash your headlamps
- [ ] steer over to the left
- [ ] check for traffic overtaking on your offside.

Answer

- [x] check for traffic overtaking on your offside

A last check in the offside mirror will allow you sight of any cyclist or motorcyclist passing on your offside.

Question

You are driving in slow-moving queues of traffic. Just before changing lane you should

Mark one answer

- [ ] sound the horn
- [ ] look for motorcyclists filtering through the traffic
- [ ] give a 'slowing down' arm signal
- [ ] change down to first gear.

Answer

- [x] look for motorcyclists filtering through the traffic

In this situation motorcyclists could be passing you on either side. Always check before you change lanes or change direction.

Question

Which of the following are a major cause of motorcycle collisions?

Mark one answer

- [ ] Car drivers.
- [ ] Moped riders.
- [ ] Sunny weather conditions.
- [ ] Traffic lights.

Answer

- [x] Car drivers.

Motorcycles might be hidden from view by other vehicles. Always be aware that a rider might be there.

Question

You are driving in town. There's a bus at the bus stop on the other side of the road. Why should you be careful?

Mark one answer

- ☒ The bus may have broken down.
- ☒ Pedestrians may come from behind the bus.
- ☒ The bus may move off suddenly.
- ☒ The bus may remain stationary.

Answer

☒ **Pedestrians may come from behind the bus.**

If you see a bus ahead watch out for pedestrians. They may not be able to see you if they're crossing behind the bus.

Question

You are riding on a country lane. You see cattle on the road. You should

Mark three answers

- ☒ slow down
- ☒ stop if necessary
- ☒ give plenty of room
- ☒ rev your engine
- ☒ sound your horn
- ☒ ride up close behind them.

Answers

☒ **slow down**

☒ **stop if necessary**

☒ **give plenty of room**

Try not to startle the animals. They can be easily frightened by noise or by traffic passing too closely.

Question

Which THREE should you do when passing sheep on a road?

Mark three answers

☒ Allow plenty of room.

☒ Drive very slowly.

☒ Pass quickly but quietly.

☒ Briefly sound your horn.

☒ Be ready to stop.

Answers

☒ **Allow plenty of room.**

☒ **Drive very slowly.**

☒ **Be ready to stop.**

If you see animals in the road ahead slow down and be ready to stop. Animals are easily frightened by

• noise

• vehicles passing too close to them.

Stop if signalled to by the person in charge. Switch off your engine if the animals are taking a long time to clear the road.

Question

How should you overtake horse riders?

Mark one answer

☒ Drive up close and overtake as soon as possible.

☒ Speed is not important but allow plenty of room.

☒ Use your horn just once to warn them.

☒ Drive slowly and leave plenty of room.

Answer

☒ **Drive slowly and leave plenty of room.**

If you're driving or riding on a country road then take extra care. Be ready for

• farm animals

• horses

• pedestrians

• farm vehicles.

Always be prepared to slow down or stop.

Question

You notice horse riders in front. What should you do FIRST?

Mark one answer

☒ Pull out to the middle of the road.

☒ Be prepared to slow down.

☒ Accelerate around them.

☒ Signal right.

Answer

☒ **Be prepared to slow down.**

When you're driving or riding you must always look well ahead and be ready to deal with hazards as they occur.

Question

As you are driving along you meet a group of horses and riders from a riding school. Why should you be extra cautious?

Mark one answer

- ☒ They will be moving in single file.
- ☒ They will be moving slowly.
- ☒ Many of the riders may be learners.
- ☒ The horses will panic more because they are in a group.

Answer

☒ **Many of the riders may be learners.**

If you see a group of horses ahead be extra cautious, especially if they're being ridden by children. The riders might be learners and may not be able to control their animals if they're startled.

Question

You are driving on a narrow country road. Where would you find it most difficult to see horses and riders ahead of you?

Mark one answer

- ☒ On left-hand bends.
- ☒ When travelling downhill.
- ☒ When travelling uphill.
- ☒ On right-hand bends.

Answer

☒ **On left-hand bends.**

You're more likely to come across horses on country roads. These roads can be narrow so extra care must be taken when approaching left-hand bends as your view of the road ahead will be restricted.

Question

A horse rider's in the left-hand lane approaching a roundabout. The driver behind should expect the rider to

Mark one answer

- ☒ go in any direction
- ☒ turn right
- ☒ turn left
- ☒ go ahead.

Answer

☒ **go in any direction**

Horses and their riders will move more slowly than other road users. They might not have time to cut across busy traffic to take up positions in the offside lane. For this reason a horse and rider may approach a roundabout in the left-hand lane, even though they're turning right.

Question

The vehicle ahead is being driven by a learner. You should

Mark one answer

- ☒ keep calm and be patient
- ☒ ride up close behind
- ☒ put your headlight on full beam
- ☒ sound your horn and overtake.

Answer

☒ **keep calm and be patient**

Learners might take longer to react to traffic situations. Don't unnerve them by riding up close behind.

Question

Which age group is most likely to be involved in a road accident?

Mark one answer

- [ ] 36 to 45-year-olds.
- [ ] 55-year-olds and over.
- [ ] 46 to 55-year-olds.
- [ ] 17 to 25-year-olds.

Answer

✖ **17 to 25-year-olds.**

Statistics show that if you're between the ages of 17 and 25 you're more likely to be involved in a road accident. There are several reasons contributing to this, but in most cases accidents are due to driver or rider error.

Question

What's the most common factor in causing road accidents?

Mark one answer

- [ ] Weather conditions.
- [ ] Driver error.
- [ ] Road conditions.
- [ ] Mechanical failure.

Answer

✖ **Driver error.**

Bad weather and different conditions will increase the risks so you must drive accordingly.

Be aware of the distance it will take you to stop

- in good conditions
- during wet or icy weather
- when you're tired
- when you don't concentrate or are distracted. (Your thinking distance will increase.)

Question

Riders are more likely to have a serious accident if they

Mark one answer

- [ ] wear glasses or contact lenses
- [ ] have recently passed their test
- [ ] are carrying pillion passengers
- [ ] haven't taken a theory test.

Answer

✖ **have recently passed their test**

It takes time to experience different situations on the road. Develop safe habits and a responsible attitude from the start. This will help you to become a better rider.

Question

You have just passed your driving test. How likely are you to have an accident, compared with other drivers?

Mark one answer

☒ More likely.

☒ It depends on your age.

☒ Less likely.

☒ About the same.

Question

How would you react to other drivers who appear to be inexperienced?

Mark one answer

☒ Sound your horn to warn them of your presence.

☒ Be patient and prepared for them to react more slowly.

☒ Flash your headlights to indicate that it's safe for them to proceed.

☒ Overtake them as soon as possible.

Question

As a new driver, how can you decrease your risk of accidents on the motorway?

Mark one answer

☒ By keeping up with the car in front.

☒ By never driving over 45 mph.

☒ By driving only in the nearside lane.

☒ By taking further training.

Answer

☒ **More likely.**

When you pass your practical driving test you'll have demonstrated that you're safe to drive or ride without supervision. It takes experience to become a good driver. Even then, try to learn from your experiences. This will increase your ability to anticipate the actions of other drivers and therefore help to make you a safer driver. Discuss further training with your Approved Driving Instructor (ADI).

Answer

☒ **Be patient and prepared for them to react more slowly.**

Learners might not have confidence when they first start to drive. Allow them plenty of room and don't react adversely to their hesitation. We all learn from experience but new drivers will have had less practice in dealing with all the situations that might occur.

Answer

☒ **By taking further training.**

You're more likely to have an accident in the first year after taking your test. Lack of experience means that you might not react to hazards as quickly as a more experienced driver or rider. Further training will help you to become safer on the roads.

If you're a motorcyclist ask your Compulsory Basic Training (CBT) instructor about this.

Question

A friend wants to teach you to drive a car. They must

Mark one answer

☒ be over 21 and have held a full licence for at least two years

☒ be over 18 and hold an advanced driver's certificate

☒ be over 18 and have fully comprehensive insurance

☒ be over 21 and have held a full licence for at least three years.

Answer

☒ **be over 21 and have held a full licence for at least three years**

Teaching someone to drive is a responsible task. You're advised to contact a qualified Approved Driving Instructor (ADI) about learning to drive. This will ensure that you're taught the correct procedures from the start.

Question

Your vehicle hits a pedestrian at 40 mph. The pedestrian will

Mark one answer

☒ certainly be killed

☒ certainly survive

☒ probably be killed

☒ probably survive.

Answer

☒ **probably be killed**

If you're a car driver ask your Approved Driving Instructor (ADI) about the Pass Plus scheme. This is a course designed to give you further instruction, which includes driving

• in town

• out of town

• in all weathers

• at night

• on dual carriageways

• on motorways.

Taking further training with a professional will help you to gain experience and positive driving skills. Taking the Pass Plus course may also provide you with cheaper insurance.

Whether driving or riding you must always be aware that there may be others on the road who are particularly vulnerable. Always be on the lookout for danger and adjust your speed accordingly.

Question

At night you see a pedestrian wearing reflective clothing and carrying a bright red light. What does this mean?

Mark one answer

☒ You are approaching roadworks.

☒ You are approaching an organised march.

☒ You are approaching a slow-moving vehicle.

☒ You are approaching an accident black spot.

Question

A pedestrian steps out into the road just ahead of you. What should you do FIRST?

Mark one answer

☒ Sound your horn.

☒ Check your mirror.

☒ Flash your headlights.

☒ Press the brake.

Answer

✖ **You are approaching an organised march.**

The people involved in the march should be keeping to the left, but this can't be assumed. Pass slowly, ensuring that you have the time to do so safely. Be aware that the pedestrians have their backs to you and might not know that you're there.

Answer

✖ **Press the brake.**

You should always react quickly to avoid a pedestrian. The normal slowing-down procedure might result in injury in this case. The vehicle behind you should have left enough room to stop safely, and you must act to protect vulnerable road users.

SECTION 7 OTHER TYPES OF VEHICLE

This section looks at the risks when dealing with
different types of vehicle.

The questions will ask you about

- motorcycles
- lorries
- buses.

Question

The road is wet. Why might a motorcyclist steer round drain covers on a bend?

Mark one answer

- ☒ To avoid puncturing the tyres on the edge of the drain covers.
- ☒ To prevent the motorcycle sliding on the metal drain covers.
- ☒ To help judge the bend using the drain covers as marker points.
- ☒ To avoid splashing pedestrians on the pavement.

Question

It is very windy. You are behind a motorcyclist who is overtaking a high-sided vehicle. What should you do?

Mark one answer

- ☒ Overtake the motorcyclist immediately.
- ☒ Keep well back.
- ☒ Stay level with the motorcyclist.
- ☒ Keep close to the motorcyclist.

Answer

☒ **To prevent the motorcycle sliding on the metal drain covers.**

The actions other drivers take may be due to the size or characteristics of their vehicle. If you understand this it will help you to anticipate their actions.

Motorcyclists will be checking the road ahead for uneven or slippery surfaces, especially in wet weather. They may need to move across their lane to avoid road surface hazards.

Answer

☒ **Keep well back.**

Motorcyclists are affected more by windy weather than other vehicles. Keep well back as they could be blown off course.

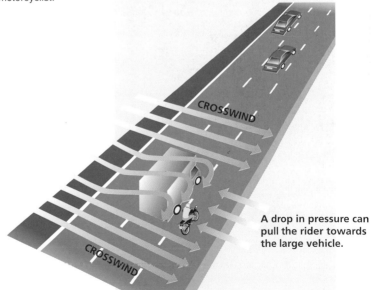

CROSSWIND

CROSSWIND

A drop in pressure can pull the rider towards the large vehicle.

Question

It is very windy. You are about to overtake a motorcyclist. You should

Mark one answer

☒ overtake slowly

☒ allow extra room

☒ sound your horn

☒ keep close as you pass.

Answer

☒ **allow extra room**

Side winds can blow a cyclist across the lane. Passing too close could also cause a draught, unsteadying the rider.

Question

Bells hanging high across the road surface are warning you

Mark one answer

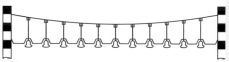

☒ that you are approaching a high bridge

☒ of overhanging trees

☒ of overhead electrified cables

☒ that you are approaching a level crossing.

Answer

☒ **of overhead electrified cables**

Check road signs as you drive. Study the traffic signs in *The Highway Code*. You can find more traffic signs in *Know Your Traffic Signs*.

Question

You are following a large articulated vehicle. It is going to turn left into a narrow road. What action should you take?

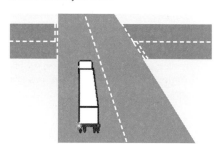

Mark one answer

☒ Move out and overtake on the offside.

☒ Pass on the left as the vehicle moves out.

☒ Be prepared to stop behind.

☒ Overtake quickly before the lorry moves out.

Answer

☒ **Be prepared to stop behind.**

Lorries are larger and longer than other vehicles. This will affect their position when approaching junctions – especially when turning left. They need more room so that they don't cut in and mount the kerb when turning.

Question
You are following a long vehicle. It approaches a crossroads and signals left, but moves out to the right. You should

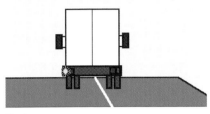

Mark one answer

- [ ] get closer in order to pass it quickly
- [ ] stay well back and give it room
- [ ] assume the signal's wrong and it's really turning right
- [ ] overtake as it starts to slow down.

Answer

☒ **stay well back and give it room**

Approaching a left turn a lorry may swing out to the right. This is to allow the rear wheels to clear the kerb as it turns. If you see a gap on the nearside don't try to filter through.

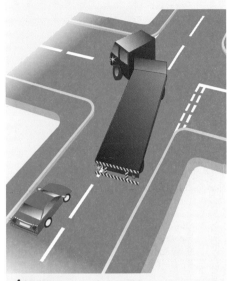

Question
You are riding behind a long vehicle. There is a mini-roundabout ahead. The vehicle is signalling left, but positioned to the right. You should

Mark one answer

- [ ] sound your horn
- [ ] overtake on the left
- [ ] keep well back
- [ ] flash your headlight.

Answer

☒ **keep well back**

The long vehicle needs more room to make the left turn. Don't overtake on the left. Staying well back will also give you a better view around the vehicle.

Question

You are following a long vehicle approaching a crossroads. The driver signals right but moves close to the left-hand kerb. What should you do?

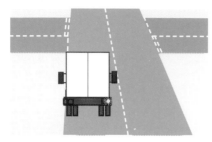

Mark one answer

- ☒ Warn the driver of the wrong signal.
- ☒ Wait behind the long vehicle.
- ☒ Report the driver to the police.
- ☒ Overtake on the right-hand side.

Answer

☒ **Wait behind the long vehicle.**

When a long vehicle is going to turn right it may need to keep close to the left-hand kerb. This is to prevent the rear end of the vehicle or trailer cutting the corner. You need to be aware of how long vehicles behave in such situations.

Don't overtake the lorry because it could turn as you're alongside. Stay behind and give it plenty of room.

Question

You are approaching a mini-roundabout. The long vehicle in front is signalling left but positioned over to the right. You should

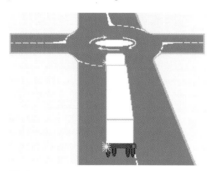

Mark one answer

- ☒ sound your horn
- ☒ overtake on the left
- ☒ follow the same course as the lorry
- ☒ keep well back.

Answer

☒ **keep well back**

At mini-roundabouts there isn't much room for a long vehicle to manoeuvre. It will have to swing out wide so that it can complete the turn safely. Keep well back and allow plenty of room. Don't drive or ride along its nearside.

Question

You are towing a caravan. Which is the safest type of rear view mirror to use?

Mark one answer

 Interior wide-angle-view mirror.

🗙 Extended-arm side mirrors.

🗙 Ordinary door mirrors.

🗙 Ordinary interior mirror.

Answer

 Extended-arm side mirrors.

Towing a large trailer or caravan can greatly reduce your view of the road. The correct equipment will help you to get a better view behind and around the unit.

Question

You keep well back while waiting to overtake a large vehicle. Another car fills the gap. You should

Mark one answer

🗙 sound your horn

🗙 drop back further

🗙 flash your headlights

🗙 start to overtake.

Answer

 drop back further

It's very frustrating when your separation distance is shortened by another car. React positively and consider your own, and your passengers', safety.

Question

Before overtaking a large vehicle you should keep well back. Why is this?

Mark one answer

🗙 To give acceleration space to overtake quickly on blind bends.

🗙 To get the best view of the road ahead.

🗙 To leave a gap in case the vehicle stops and rolls back.

🗙 To offer other drivers a safe gap if they want to overtake you.

Answer

🗙 **To get the best view of the road ahead.**

When following a large vehicle keep well back. If you're too close

• you won't be able to see the road ahead

• the driver of the long vehicle might not be able to see you in his mirrors.

Question
You wish to overtake a long, slow-moving vehicle on a busy road. You should

Mark one answer

- ☒ wait behind until the driver waves you past
- ☒ flash your headlights for the oncoming traffic to give way
- ☒ follow it closely and keep moving out to see the road ahead
- ☒ keep well back until you can see that it is clear.

Answer
☒ **keep well back until you can see that it is clear**

If you wish to overtake a long vehicle stay well back so that you can see the road ahead. Don't

- get up close to the vehicle – this will restrict your view of the road ahead
- get impatient – overtaking on a busy road calls for sound judgement
- take a gamble – only overtake when you can see that you can safely complete the manoeuvre
- flash your headlights – this could confuse and mislead other traffic
- sound your horn.

Question
You are driving downhill. There is a car parked on the other side of the road. Large, slow lorries are coming towards you. You should

Mark one answer

- ☒ keep going because you have the right of way
- ☒ slow down and give way
- ☒ speed up and get past quickly
- ☒ pull over on the right behind the parked car.

Answer
☒ **slow down and give way**

Large vehicles need several gear changes to build up speed and this takes time, especially on an uphill gradient. You should keep this in mind and give way so that they can maintain momentum up the hill.

Question
When about to overtake a long vehicle you should

Mark one answer

- ☒ sound the horn to warn the driver that you're there
- ☒ stay well back from the lorry to obtain a better view
- ☒ drive close to the lorry in order to pass more quickly
- ☒ flash your lights and wait for the driver to signal when it is safe.

Answer
☒ **stay well back from the lorry to obtain a better view**

If you're thinking about overtaking ask yourself if it's really necessary. An unladen large vehicle can make surprisingly good progress.

Question

The FIRST thing you should do when you want to overtake a large lorry is

Mark one answer

☒ move close behind so that you can pass quickly

☒ keep in close to the left-hand side

☒ flash your headlights and wait for the driver to wave you on

☒ stay well back to get a better view.

Answer

☒ **stay well back to get a better view**

When you're planning to overtake a large vehicle take its length into account. It will take you longer to pass a lorry or coach than another car. You'll need to look further ahead.

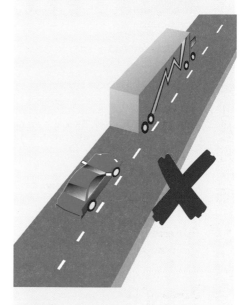

Question

Why is passing a lorry more risky than passing a car?

Mark one answer

☒ Lorries are longer than cars.

☒ Lorries may suddenly pull up.

☒ The brakes of lorries are not as good.

☒ Lorries climb hills more slowly.

Answer

☒ **Lorries are longer than cars.**

Hazards to watch for include

• oncoming traffic

• junctions

• bends or dips, which could restrict your view

• any signs or road markings prohibiting overtaking.

Never begin to overtake unless you can see that it's safe to complete the manoeuvre.

Question

You're driving along a road and you see this signal. It means

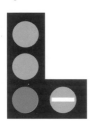

Mark one answer

- ☒ cars must stop
- ☒ trams must stop
- ☒ both trams and cars must stop
- ☒ both trams and cars can continue.

Answer

☒ **trams must stop**

Trams are popular in some cities, not least because they don't create fumes so they're cleaner. You may not live in an area that has trams but you should still learn the signs. You never know when you might drive through a town that has them.

Question

You are travelling behind a bus that pulls up at a bus stop. What should you do?

Mark two answers

- ☒ Accelerate past the bus sounding your horn.
- ☒ Watch carefully for pedestrians.
- ☒ Be ready to give way to the bus.
- ☒ Pull in closely behind the bus.

Answer

☒ **Watch carefully for pedestrians.**

☒ **Be ready to give way to the bus.**

There might be pedestrians crossing from in front of the bus. Look out for them if you intend to pass. Consider staying back and waiting.

How many people are waiting to get on the bus? Check the queue if you can. The bus might be moving off straight away.

Question
When you approach a bus signalling to move off from a bus stop you should

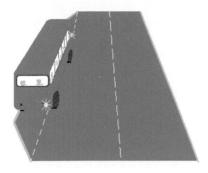

Answer

☒ **allow it to pull away, if it is safe to do so**

Give way to buses whenever you can do so safely, especially when they signal to pull away from bus stops. Look out for people who've got off the bus and may try to cross the road. Don't

- try to accelerate past before it moves away
- flash your lights – other road users may be misled by this signal.

Mark one answer

☒ get past before it moves

☒ allow it to pull away, if it is safe to do so

☒ flash your headlamps as you approach

☒ signal left and wave the bus on.

Question
In which THREE places could a strong crosswind affect your course?

Mark three answers

☒ After overtaking a large vehicle.

☒ When passing gaps in hedges.

☒ On exposed sections of roadway.

☒ In towns.

☒ In tunnels.

☒ When passing parked vehicles.

Answers

☒ **After overtaking a large vehicle.**

☒ **When passing gaps in hedges.**

☒ **On exposed sections of roadway.**

Crosswinds affect some vehicles more than others. The worst affected vehicles are

- high-sided vehicles
- caravans
- motorcycles
- cycles.

It's important to be aware which types of vehicles are affected so that you can anticipate their actions.

Question

Which of these vehicles is LEAST likely to be affected by crosswinds?

Mark one answer

☒ Cyclists.

☒ Motorcyclists.

☒ High-sided vehicles.

☒ Cars.

Answer

 Cars.

Crosswinds can take you by surprise

• after overtaking a large vehicle

• when passing gaps between hedges or buildings

• on exposed sections of road.

Question

What does 'tailgating' mean?

Mark one answer

☒ When a vehicle delivering goods has its tailgate down.

☒ When a vehicle is travelling with its back doors open.

☒ When a driver is following another vehicle too closely.

☒ When stationary vehicles are too close in a queue.

Answer

☒ **When a driver is following another vehicle too closely.**

This can often be seen on motorways, when traffic is travelling at high speeds. Tailgating is a highly dangerous practice and could lead to a serious multiple accident.

Question

You are following a large lorry on a wet road. Spray makes it difficult to see. You should

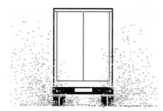

Mark one answer

☒ drop back until you can see better

☒ put your headlights on full beam

☒ keep close to the lorry, away from the spray

☒ speed up and overtake quickly.

Answer

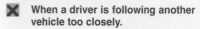 **drop back until you can see better**

In the wet, large vehicles may throw up a lot of spray. This will make it difficult to see ahead. Dropping back further will

• move you out of the spray and so allow you to see further

• increase your separation distance. It takes longer to stop in the wet and you need to allow more room.

Don't

• get up close behind

• overtake, unless you can see the way ahead is clear.

Question

You are driving on a wet motorway with surface spray. You should

Mark one answer

☒ use your hazard flashers

☒ use dipped headlights

☒ use your rear fog lights

☒ drive in any lane with no traffic.

Answer

☒ **use dipped headlights**

When surface spray reduces visibility switch on your dipped headlights. This will help other road users to see you.

This section looks at the handling of your vehicle in different conditions.

The questions will ask you about

- weather conditions
- road conditions
- the time of day
- speed
- traffic calming.

Question

You should not drive with your foot on the clutch for longer than necessary because it

Mark one answer

- [ ] increases wear on the gearbox
- [ ] increases petrol consumption
- [ ] reduces your control of the vehicle
- [ ] reduces the grip of the tyres.

Question

You should not ride with your clutch in for longer than necessary because it

Mark one answer

- [ ] increases wear on the gearbox
- [ ] increases petrol consumption
- [ ] reduces your control of the motorcycle
- [ ] reduces the grip of the tyres.

Question

What are TWO main reasons why coasting downhill is wrong?

Mark two answers

- [ ] Petrol consumption will be higher.
- [ ] The vehicle will pick up speed.
- [ ] It puts more wear and tear on the tyres.
- [ ] You have less braking and steering control.
- [ ] It damages the engine.

Answer

✗ reduces your control of the vehicle

Pressing down the clutch pedal or riding with the clutch in for longer than necessary is referred to as coasting. Coasting your vehicle or machine will

- cause the vehicle or machine to pick up speed
- give you less steering and braking control
- make selecting the correct gear difficult.

Answer

✗ reduces your control of the motorcycle

Coasting

- gives you less steering control
- reduces the traction on the road surface
- causes the machine to pick up speed.

If you're travelling downhill your machine will gather speed quickly. The engine won't be able to assist the braking.

Answers

✗ The vehicle will pick up speed.

✗ You have less braking and steering control.

It's especially important that you don't coast your vehicle

- at junctions
- approaching hazards
- on bends.

Question
Why is coasting wrong?

Mark one answer

- ☒ It will cause the car to skid.
- ☒ It will make the engine stall.
- ☒ The engine will run faster.
- ☒ There is no engine braking.

Answer

☒ **There is no engine braking.**

Try to look ahead and read the road. Plan your approach to junctions and select the correct gear in good time. This will give you the control you need to deal with any hazards that occur.

You'll coast a little every time you change gear. This can't be avoided but it should be kept to a minimum.

Question
Which THREE of the following will affect your stopping distance?

Mark three answers

- ☒ How fast you are going.
- ☒ The tyres on your vehicle.
- ☒ The time of day.
- ☒ The weather.
- ☒ The street lighting.

Answers

☒ **How fast you are going.**

☒ **The tyres on your vehicle.**

☒ **The weather.**

You should be aware that there are several factors that can affect the distance it takes to stop your vehicle.

Your stopping distance in wet weather will increase. You should double the separation distance from the car in front. Your tyres will have less grip on the road and therefore need more time to stop. Always drive in accordance with the conditions.

Question
You are approaching a bend at speed. You should begin to brake

Mark one answer

- ☒ on the bend
- ☒ after the bend
- ☒ after changing gears
- ☒ before the bend.

Answer

☒ **before the bend**

Full control of the vehicle is essential at all times. Adjust your speed before the bend. Change gear if necessary and drive round it under gentle acceleration.

Question

You are following a vehicle at a safe distance on a wet road. Another driver overtakes you and pulls into the gap you have left. What should you do?

Mark one answer

☒ Flash your headlights as a warning.

☒ Try to overtake safely as soon as you can.

☒ Drop back to regain a safe distance.

☒ Stay close to the other vehicle until it moves on.

Question

Why is pressing the clutch down for long periods a bad habit?

Mark one answer

☒ It reduces the car's speed when going downhill.

☒ It causes the engine to wear out more quickly.

☒ It reduces the driver's control of the vehicle.

☒ It causes the engine to use more fuel.

Question

You should avoid 'coasting' your vehicle because it could

Mark one answer

☒ damage the suspension

☒ increase tyre wear

☒ flatten the battery

☒ reduce steering control.

Answer

❌ **Drop back to regain a safe distance.**

The weather will affect the way your vehicle or machine behaves. It will increase the time it takes for you to stop and can affect your control.

Drive at a speed that will allow you to stop safely and in good time.

If another vehicle pulls into the gap you've left ease back until you've regained your stopping distance. Don't flash your lights or drive up close to it.

Answer

❌ **It reduces the driver's control of the vehicle.**

'Coasting' means that although your vehicle or machine is moving it isn't being driven by the engine. This could be because

• the clutch is down or being held in

• the vehicle or machine isn't in gear (i.e., it's in neutral).

Answer

❌ **reduce steering control**

Coasting your vehicle or machine will

• cause it to pick up speed

• give you less steering and braking control

• make selecting the correct gear difficult.

Question

You are driving in the left-hand lane of a dual carriageway. Another vehicle overtakes and pulls in front of you leaving you without enough separation distance. You should

Mark one answer

☒ move to the right lane

☒ continue as you are

☒ drop back

☒ sound your horn.

Answer

☒ **drop back**

Dual carriageways have at least two lanes in each direction. There will be a central reserve where there may be a safety barrier.

If you're overtaken by another vehicle and it cuts in too closely don't react by flashing your lights or giving any other signal. Gradually increase your distance from the vehicle so that you have a safe gap if you need to stop.

Question

You are driving on the motorway in windy conditions. When passing high-sided vehicles you should

Mark one answer

☒ increase your speed

☒ be wary of a sudden gust

☒ drive alongside very closely

☒ expect normal conditions.

Answer

☒ **be wary of a sudden gust**

The draught caused by other vehicles could be strong enough to push you out of your lane. Keep both hands on the steering wheel to maintain full control.

Question

You wish to overtake on a dual carriageway. You see in your mirror that the car behind has pulled out to overtake you. You should

Mark one answer

☒ not signal until the car has passed

☒ signal and pull out to overtake

☒ signal to tell the driver behind that you also want to overtake

☒ touch the brakes to show your brake lights.

Answer

☒ **not signal until the car has passed**

Before you overtake ask yourself, 'Is it really necessary?'

Look well ahead to check for hazards. Check in your mirror. If there's a vehicle about to overtake you, wait until it's passed before you signal to pull out. Then do so safely.

Question

In which THREE of these situations may you overtake another vehicle on the left?

Mark three answers

☒ When you are in a one-way street.

☒ When approaching a motorway slip road where you will be turning off.

☒ When the vehicle in front is signalling to turn right.

☒ When a slower vehicle is travelling in the right-hand lane of a dual carriageway.

☒ In slow-moving traffic queues when traffic in the right-hand lane is moving more slowly.

Question

How should you drive around a bend on ice?

Mark one answer

☒ Using the clutch and brake together.

☒ In first gear.

☒ Braking as you enter the bend.

☒ Slowly and smoothly.

Question

Give two reasons for using an additive in the windscreen washer reservoir.

Mark two answers

☒ To prevent freezing in winter.

☒ To wipe off leaves in autumn.

☒ To help prevent mould growth.

☒ To clear dead insects in summer.

☒ To prevent corrosion.

Answers

✖ **When you are in a one-way street.**

✖ **When the vehicle in front is signalling to turn right.**

✖ **In slow-moving traffic queues when traffic in the right-hand lane is moving more slowly.**

At certain times of the day traffic might be heavy. If traffic is moving in queues and vehicles in the right-hand lane are moving more slowly you may overtake on the left. Don't keep changing lanes to try and beat the queue.

Answer

✖ **Slowly and smoothly.**

When the weather is cold and the roads are icy you must be aware that your vehicle or machine will handle differently. The tyres will loose much of their grip on the road, which will greatly affect your steering control. If you're driving around bends in icy weather do so slowly and smoothly.

Answer

✖ **To prevent freezing in winter.**

✖ **To clear dead insects in summer.**

Make sure that your washers are working, and keep the reservoir filled. It's important that you maintain full vision through the windscreen.

Question

You're approaching this junction. As the motorcyclist you should

Mark two answers

- ☒ prepare to slow down
- ☒ sound your horn
- ☒ keep near the left kerb
- ☒ speed up to clear the junction
- ☒ stop, as the car has right of way.

Question

Which FOUR types of road surface increase the risk of skidding for motorcyclists?

Mark four answers

- ☒ White lining.
- ☒ Dry tarmac.
- ☒ Tar banding.
- ☒ Yellow grid lining.
- ☒ Loose chippings.

Answers

- ☒ **prepare to slow down**
- ☒ **sound your horn**

Look out for road signs indicating side roads, even if you aren't turning off. A driver emerging might not be able to see you due to parked cars or heavy traffic. Always be prepared, and stop if it's necessary. Remember, no one has priority at unmarked crossroads.

Answers

- ☒ **White lining.**
- ☒ **Tar banding.**
- ☒ **Yellow grid lining.**
- ☒ **Loose chippings.**

If you're riding a motorcycle you must look at the road surface ahead. The stability of your machine will depend on it. Also, look out for

- pot-holes
- drain covers (especially in the wet)
- oily surfaces
- road markings
- tram tracks
- wet mud and leaves.

Question
Which THREE of these can cause skidding?

Mark three answers

- ☒ Braking too gently.
- ☒ Leaning too far over when cornering.
- ☒ Staying upright when cornering.
- ☒ Braking too hard.
- ☒ Changing direction suddenly.

Question
It is very cold and the road looks wet. You cannot hear any road noise. You should

Mark two answers

- ☒ continue riding at the same speed
- ☒ ride slower in as high a gear as possible
- ☒ ride in as low a gear as possible
- ☒ keep revving your engine
- ☒ slow down as there may be black ice.

Question
You are approaching a road with a surface of loose chippings. What should you do?

Mark one answer

- ☒ Ride normally.
- ☒ Speed up.
- ☒ Slow down.
- ☒ Stop.

Answers

- ☒ **Leaning too far over when cornering.**
- ☒ **Braking too hard.**
- ☒ **Changing direction suddenly.**

In order to keep control of your vehicle and prevent skidding you must plan well ahead to prevent harsh, late braking. Take the road and weather conditions into consideration and ride accordingly.

Answer

- ☒ **ride slower in as high a gear as possible**
- ☒ **slow down as there may be black ice**

Rain freezing on roads as it falls is called black ice and isn't clearly visible. The first indication that you might have of it is when the steering becomes very light. You need to keep your speed down and ride according to the weather conditions.

Answer

- ☒ **Slow down.**

You should

- ride at an appropriate speed
- apply both front and rear brakes evenly
- brake when travelling in a straight line and your machine is upright.

Don't make sudden changes of direction unless you are avoiding an accident.

The handling of your machine will be greatly affected by the road surface that you're riding on. Look at the road ahead and be alert if the road looks uneven or has loose chippings. Slow down in good time – braking harshly here will cause you to skid.

Question

When snow is falling heavily you should

Mark one answer

- ☒ drive as long as your headlights are used
- ☒ not drive unless you have a mobile phone
- ☒ drive only when your journey is short
- ☒ not drive unless it's essential.

Answer

☒ **not drive unless it's essential**

Consider if the increased risk is worth it. If the weather conditions are bad and your journey isn't essential then stay at home.

Question

How can you best control your vehicle when driving in snow?

Mark one answer

- ☒ By driving slowly in as high a gear as possible.
- ☒ By staying in low gear and gripping the steering wheel tightly.
- ☒ By driving in first gear.
- ☒ By keeping the engine revs high and slipping the clutch.

Answer

☒ **By driving slowly in as high a gear as possible.**

If the ground is covered with snow move off in as high a gear as possible. This will lessen the chance of skidding by reducing the power to the driven wheels.

Question

You are driving on an icy road. What distance should you drive from the car in front?

Mark one answer

- ☒ Eight times the normal distance.
- ☒ Six times the normal distance.
- ☒ Ten times the normal distance.
- ☒ Four times the normal distance.

Answer

☒ **Ten times the normal distance.**

Think about how far this is. It's a long way; probably further than you think.

Question

To correct a rear-wheel skid you should

Mark one answer

☒ not turn at all

☒ turn away from it

☒ turn into it

☒ apply your handbrake.

Answer

☒ **turn into it**

Prevention is better than cure so it's important that you take every precaution to prevent a skid. If you do feel your vehicle beginning to skid try to steer to recover control. Don't brake suddenly – this will only make the situation worse.

Question

You are driving in very wet weather. Your vehicle begins to slide. This effect is called

Mark one answer

☒ hosing

☒ weaving

☒ aquaplaning

☒ fading.

Answer

☒ **aquaplaning**

Water can build up between the tyres and the road. This means that the tyres might not have contact with the road. Your vehicle could slide on the film of water, causing the steering to feel light and you to lose proper control.

Question

Why should you test your brakes after this hazard?

Mark one answer

☒ Because you will be driving on a slippery road.

☒ Because your brakes will be soaking wet.

☒ Because you will have driven down a long hill.

☒ Because you will have just crossed a long bridge.

Answer

☒ **Because your brakes will be soaking wet.**

A ford is a crossing over a stream that's shallow enough to drive through. If you've driven through a ford or a deep puddle the water can affect your brakes. Be sure you check that they're working before returning to normal speed.

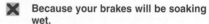

Question

You have to make a journey in fog. What are the TWO most important things you should do before you set out?

Mark two answers

- [ ] Top up the radiator with antifreeze.
- [ ] Make sure that you have a warning triangle in the vehicle.
- [x] Check that your lights are working.
- [ ] Check the battery.
- [x] Make sure that the windows are clean.

Answers

- [x] Check that your lights are working.
- [x] Make sure that the windows are clean.

Don't drive in fog unless you really have to. Drive in accordance with the conditions.

Question

You have to make a journey in fog. What are the TWO most important things you should do before you set out?

Mark two answers

- [ ] Fill up with fuel.
- [ ] Make sure that you have a warm drink with you.
- [x] Check that your lights are working.
- [ ] Check the battery.
- [x] Make sure that your visor is clean.

Answers

- [x] Check that your lights are working.
- [x] Make sure that your visor is clean.

If you're riding a motorcycle keep your visor as clean as possible to give you a clear view of the road. It's a good idea to carry a clean, damp cloth in a polythene bag for this purpose. When the weather is foggy or misty ensure that your lights are clean and can be seen clearly by other road users.

Question

You have to make a journey in foggy conditions. You should

Mark one answer

- [ ] follow closely other vehicles' tail lights
- [ ] never use demisters and windscreen wipers
- [ ] leave plenty of time for your journey
- [ ] keep two seconds behind other vehicles.

Answer

- [x] leave plenty of time for your journey

If you're planning to make a journey in foggy conditions listen to the weather reports on the radio or television. Don't drive if visibility is very low or your journey isn't necessary. If you do travel, leave plenty of time for your journey. If there's someone expecting you at the other end of your journey let them know that you'll be taking longer than normal to arrive. Take your time and don't hurry.

Question

You are following other vehicles in fog with your lights on. How else can you reduce the chances of being involved in an accident?

Mark one answer

- ☒ Keep close to the vehicle in front.
- ☒ Use your main beam instead of dipped headlights.
- ☒ Keep together with the faster vehicles.
- ☒ Reduce your speed and increase the gap.

Answer

☒ **Reduce your speed and increase the gap.**

Always ensure that you have your lights on and that you're seen by all other road users. Use dipped headlights. If visibility is below 100 metres (330 feet) use fog lights and high-intensity rear lights. Drive at a sensible speed and don't follow the car in front too closely. You'll need to adjust your stopping distance as the road is likely to be wet and slippery.

Question

Why should you always reduce your speed when driving in fog?

Mark one answer

- ☒ Because the brakes do not work as well.
- ☒ Because you could be dazzled by other people's fog lights.
- ☒ Because the engine's colder.
- ☒ Because it is more difficult to see events ahead.

Answer

☒ **Because it is more difficult to see events ahead.**

Driving in fog is hazardous. Only travel out if it's really necessary. To drive or ride safely you must always look well ahead. In fog this won't be possible and you'll have less time to react to any hazards. You must reduce your speed.

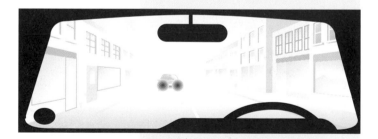

Question

You are driving in fog. The car behind seems to be very close. You should

Mark one answer

- ☒ switch on your hazard warning lights
- ☒ pull over and stop immediately
- ☒ speed up to get away
- ☒ continue cautiously.

Answer

☒ **continue cautiously**

If the car behind seems to be too close to you, the driver's probably using your rear lights as a guide through the fog. This isn't advisable. A good separation distance will be even more important on a wet road surface. Don't react to this but continue cautiously.

Question

You are driving in fog. Why should you keep well back from the vehicle in front?

Mark one answer

☒ In case it changes direction suddenly.

☒ In case its fog lights dazzle you.

☒ In case it stops suddenly.

☒ In case its brake lights dazzle you.

Answer

☒ **In case it stops suddenly.**

If you're following another road user in fog stay well back. The driver in front won't be able to see hazards until they're close and might brake suddenly. You'll need a good separation distance as the road surface is likely to be wet and slippery.

Question

You should switch your rear fog lights on when visibility drops below

Mark one answer

☒ your overall stopping distance

☒ ten car lengths

☒ 10 metres (33 feet)

☒ 100 metres (330 feet).

Answer

☒ **100 metres (330 feet)**

This will help other road users to see you. Don't forget to turn off fog lights once visibility is clear. Their brightness might be mistaken for brake lights.

Question

You are driving in poor visibility. You can see more than 100 metres (330 feet) ahead. How can you make sure that other drivers can see you?

Mark one answer

☒ Turn on your dipped headlights.

☒ Follow the vehicle in front closely.

☒ Turn on your rear fog lights.

☒ Keep well out towards the middle of the road.

Answer

☒ **Turn on your dipped headlights.**

You should always use your headlights in fog. They should be on dipped beam to prevent the light reflecting back off the fog.

Question

You should only use rear fog lights when you cannot see further than about

Mark one answer

☒ 100 metres (330 feet)

☒ 200 metres (660 feet)

☒ 250 metres (800 feet)

☒ 150 metres (495 feet).

Answer

☒ **100 metres (330 feet)**

This will help other road users to see you. Don't forget to switch them off when visability improves. Driving with them on at other times, such as in heavy rain, can dazzle the car behind.

Question

Whilst driving, the fog clears and you can see more clearly. You must remember to

Mark one answer

- ☒ switch off the fog lights
- ☒ reduce your speed
- ☒ switch off the demister
- ☒ close any open windows.

Answer

☒ **switch off the fog lights**

Bright rear fog lights might be mistaken for brake lights and could be misleading for the traffic behind.

Question

You have to park on the road in fog. You should

Mark one answer

- ☒ leave sidelights on
- ☒ leave dipped headlights and fog lights on
- ☒ leave dipped headlights on
- ☒ leave main beam headlights on.

Answer

☒ **leave sidelights on**

If you have to park your vehicle in foggy conditions it's important that it can be seen by other road users.

Try to find a place to park off the road. If this isn't possible leave it facing in the same direction as the traffic. Make sure that your lights are clean and that you leave your sidelights on.

Question

On a foggy day you unavoidably have to park your car on the road. You should

Mark one answer

- ☒ leave your headlights on
- ☒ leave your fog lights on
- ☒ leave your sidelights on
- ☒ leave your hazard lights on.

Answer

☒ **leave your sidelights on**

Ensure that your vehicle can be seen by other traffic. If possible, park your car off the road in a car park or driveway to avoid the extra risk to other road users.

Question

The best place to park your motorcycle is

Mark one answer

- ☒ on soft tarmac
- ☒ on bumpy ground
- ☒ on grass
- ☒ on firm, level ground.

Answer

 on firm, level ground

Parking your machine on soft ground might cause the stand to sink and the bike to fall over. The ground should also be even and level to ensure that the bike is stable. If possible, park your machine off the road.

Question

You are driving on a motorway in fog. The left-hand edge of the motorway can be identified by reflective studs. What colour are they?

Mark one answer

- ☒ Green.
- ☒ Amber.
- ☒ Red.
- ☒ White.

Question

In normal riding your position on the road should be

Mark one answer

- ☒ about a foot from the kerb
- ☒ about central in your lane
- ☒ on the right of your lane
- ☒ near the centre of the road.

Question

You are driving on a well-lit motorway at night. You must

Mark one answer

- ☒ use only your sidelights
- ☒ always use your headlights
- ☒ always use rear fog lights
- ☒ use headlights only in bad weather.

Answer

 ☒ **Red.**

Be especially careful if you're driving on a motorway in fog. You must be able to stop well within the distance that you can see to be clear. Keep in the left-hand lane.

Reflective studs are used on motorways to help you in poor visibility. The studs are coloured so that you'll know which lane you're in and where slip roads join or leave the motorway.

Answer

☒ **about central in your lane**

If you're riding a motorcycle it's very important to ride where other road users can see you. In normal weather you should ride in the centre of your lane. This will

- help you to be seen in the mirror of the vehicle in front
- avoid uneven road surfaces in the gutter
- allow others to overtake on the right if they wish.

Answer

☒ **always use your headlights**

If you're driving on a motorway at night you must always use your headlights, even if the road is well lit. The vehicles in front must be able to see you in their mirrors.

Question

You are driving on a motorway at night. You MUST have your headlights switched on unless

Mark one answer

- there are vehicles close in front of you
- you are travelling below 50 mph
- the motorway is lit
- your vehicle is broken down on the hard shoulder.

Answer

✗ your vehicle is broken down on the hard shoulder

Always use your headlights at night on a motorway unless you're stopped on the hard shoulder. If you break down and have to stop on the hard shoulder switch off the main beam. Leave the sidelights on so that other road users can see your vehicle or machine.

Question

You are travelling on a motorway at night with other vehicles just ahead of you. Which lights should you have on?

Mark one answer

- Front fog lights.
- Main beam headlights.
- Sidelights only.
- Dipped headlights.

Answer

✗ Dipped headlights.

If you're driving or riding behind other traffic at night on the motorway

- leave a two-second time gap
- dip your headlights.

Full beam will dazzle the driver ahead. Your light beam should fall short of the vehicle in front.

Question

Which TWO of the following are correct? When overtaking at night you should

Mark two answers

- wait until a bend so that you can see the oncoming headlights
- sound your horn twice before moving out
- be careful because you can see less
- beware of bends in the road ahead
- put headlights on full beam.

Answers

✗ be careful because you can see less

✗ beware of bends in the road ahead

Only overtake the vehicle in front if it's really necessary. At night the risks are increased due to the poor visibility. Don't overtake if there's a possibility of

- road junctions
- bends ahead
- the brow of a bridge or hill, except on a dual carriageway
- pedestrian crossings
- double white lines ahead
- vehicles changing direction
- any other potential hazard.

Question
You are overtaking a car at night. You must be sure that

Mark one answer

- [x] you flash your headlamps before overtaking
- [x] your rear fog lights are switched on
- [x] you have switched your lights to full beam before overtaking
- [x] you do not dazzle other road users.

Answer
 you do not dazzle other road users

If you wish to overtake at night ensure that your lights don't reflect in the mirror of the car in front. Wait until you've overtaken before switching to full beam.

Question
You are driving at night. Why should you be extra careful of your speed?

Mark one answer

- [x] Because you might need to stop within the distance that you can see.
- [x] Because it uses more petrol.
- [x] Because driving with the lights on runs down the battery.
- [x] Because you may be late.

Answer
 Because you might need to stop within the distance that you can see.

You can't see as far at night as in daylight. Therefore, you need to be aware that you can't safely drive as fast at night. There will be more unseen hazards.

Question
When riding at night you should

Mark two answers

- [x] wear fluorescent clothing
- [x] ride closer to the vehicle in front
- [x] keep your goggles or visor clean
- [x] ride well to the left
- [x] use your headlights.

Answers
 **keep your goggles or visor clean**

use your headlights

Always make sure that you can see clearly and that other road users can see you. Make sure that your visor or goggles don't have any scratches, which might distort your view or cause dazzle. Wearing bright clothing is a good idea, but remember, only **reflective** clothing will adequately show up at night.

Question

You are travelling at night. You are dazzled by headlights coming towards you. You should

Mark one answer

- ☒ pull down your sun visor
- ☒ slow down or stop
- ☒ switch on your main beam headlights
- ☒ put your hand over your eyes.

Question

You are dazzled by oncoming headlights when driving at night. What should you do?

Mark one answer

- ☒ Slow down or stop.
- ☒ Brake hard.
- ☒ Drive faster past the oncoming car.
- ☒ Flash your lights.

Answer

☒ **slow down or stop**

If you're driving at night there will be extra hazards to deal with. The lights of oncoming vehicles can often distract. If you're dazzled by them don't

- close your eyes
- flash your headlights. This will only distract the other driver too.

Answer

☒ **Slow down or stop.**

Let your eyes readjust. Speed and distance are more difficult to judge at night. You won't be able to see as far as in daylight so less information will be available. Don't take risks, especially if you're considering overtaking the vehicle in front.

Question

When driving towards a bright setting sun, glare can be reduced by

Mark one answer

☒ closing one eye

☒ dipping the interior mirror

☒ wearing dark glasses

☒ looking sideways.

Answer

 ☒ **wearing dark glasses**

Dark glasses are often used as a fashion item but they do have their practical uses. Low sun in the early morning or evening can dazzle and distract. Lessen the risk by reducing the glare. Wear dark glasses if they help you to see better.

Question

You are on a narrow road at night. A slower-moving vehicle ahead has been signalling right for some time. What should you do?

Mark one answer

☒ Overtake on the left.

☒ Flash your headlights before overtaking.

☒ Signal right and sound your horn.

☒ Wait for the signal to be cancelled before overtaking.

Answer

☒ **Wait for the signal to be cancelled before overtaking.**

If the vehicle in front has been indicating right for some time, but has made no attempt to turn, wait for the signal to be cancelled. The other driver may have misjudged the distance to the road junction or there might be a hidden hazard. Don't

• flash your headlights

• sound your horn

• overtake without being able to see well down the road.

Question

A rumble device is designed to

Mark two answers

☒ give directions

☒ prevent cattle escaping

☒ alert drivers to low tyre pressure

☒ alert drivers to a hazard

☒ encourage drivers to reduce speed.

Answers

☒ **alert drivers to a hazard**

☒ **encourage drivers to reduce speed**

A rumble device is usually raised markings or strips on the road's surface. These strips are in places where traffic has constantly ignored warning or restriction signs. They're there for a good reason. Slow down and be ready to deal with a hazard.

Question

Which TWO are correct? The passing places on a single-track road are

Mark two answers

- ☒ for taking a rest from driving
- ☒ to pull into if an oncoming vehicle wants to proceed
- ☒ for stopping and checking your route
- ☒ to turn the car around in, if you are lost
- ☒ to pull into if the car behind wants to overtake.

Question

You see a vehicle coming towards you on a single-track road. You should

Mark one answer

- ☒ stop at a passing place
- ☒ reverse back to the main road
- ☒ do an emergency stop
- ☒ put on your hazard flashers.

Answers

- ☒ **to pull into if an oncoming vehicle wants to proceed**
- ☒ **to pull into if the car behind wants to overtake**

If you're driving on a single-track road be prepared to pull over and let other road users pass. There are passing places to enable you to do this. These shouldn't be used for parking or turning your car around.

Answer

- ☒ **stop at a passing place**

You must take extra care when driving on single-track roads. You may not be able to see around bends due to high hedges or fences. Drive with caution and expect to meet oncoming vehicles around the next bend. If you do, pull over into or opposite a passing place.

This section looks at motorway rules.

The questions will ask you about

- speed limits
- lane discipline
- stopping
- lighting
- parking.

Question

Which of the following CAN travel on a motorway?

Mark one answer

☒ Cyclists.

☒ Vans.

☒ Farm tractors.

☒ Learner drivers.

Question

As a provisional licence-holder you should not drive a car

Mark one answer

☒ over 50 mph

☒ at night

☒ on the motorway

☒ with passengers in rear seats.

Question

Which FOUR of these must not use motorways?

Mark four answers

☒ Learner car drivers.

☒ Motorcycles over 50cc.

☒ Double-decker buses.

☒ Farm tractors.

☒ Horse riders.

☒ Cyclists.

Answer

✖ **Vans.**

Motorways are designed to help traffic travel quickly. Traffic can only travel safely at high speed if the road is clear. Any slow-moving road user would be a danger to themselves and passing traffic. For this reason there are restrictions on who can use the motorway.

Answer

✖ **on the motorway**

When you've passed your practical test ask your instructor to take you for a lesson on the motorway. You'll need to get used to the speed of traffic and how to deal with multiple lanes.

Answers

✖ **Learner car drivers.**

✖ **Farm tractors.**

✖ **Horse riders.**

✖ **Cyclists.**

In addition, motorways MUST NOT be used by

• pedestrians

• motorcycles under 50cc

• certain slow-moving vehicles, without permission

• invalid carriages not weighing more than 254kg (560 lbs).

Question
Which FOUR of these must NOT use motorways?

Mark four answers

☒ Learner car drivers.

☒ Motorcycles over 50cc.

☒ Double-decker buses.

☒ Farm tractors.

☒ Learner motorcyclists.

☒ Cyclists.

Answers

☒ Learner car drivers.

☒ Farm tractors.

☒ Learner motorcyclists.

☒ Cyclists.

When you've passed your practical driving test it's a good idea to have some lessons on motorway driving. Statistically, motorways are safer than other roads, but they have rules that you need to know before you venture out for the first time. Check with your CBT instructor about this.

Question
A motorcycle is not allowed on a motorway if it has an engine size smaller than

Mark one answer

☒ 50cc

☒ 125cc

☒ 150cc

☒ 250cc.

Answer

 50cc

The restricted speed of a small machine will cause a hazard to other motorway users. If you're riding a machine with a small engine choose another route.

Question
To ride on a motorway your motorcycle must be over

Mark one answer

☒ 100cc

☒ 125cc

☒ 250cc

☒ 50cc.

Answer

 50cc

Traffic on motorways travels at high speeds. Vehicles need to be capable of keeping up with the flow of traffic. For this reason low-powered vehicles are prohibited.

Question
Why is it particularly important to carry out a check on your vehicle before making a long motorway journey?

Mark one answer

☒ You will have to do more harsh braking on motorways.

☒ Motorway service stations do not deal with breakdowns.

☒ The road surface will wear down the tyres faster.

☒ Continuous high speeds may increase the risk of your vehicle breaking down.

Answer

 Continuous high speeds may increase the risk of your vehicle breaking down.

Before you start your journey make sure that your vehicle can cope with the demands of high-speed driving. Before starting a motorway journey check your vehicle's

• oil

• water

• tyres.

Plan your rest stops if you're travelling a long way.

Question
Immediately after joining a motorway you should normally

Mark one answer

- ☒ try to overtake
- ☒ readjust your mirrors
- ☒ position your vehicle in the centre lane
- ☒ keep in the left lane.

Answer

☒ **keep in the left lane**

Wait until you've built up speed and only move into the centre lane if you intend to overtake.

Question
You are joining a motorway. Why is it important to make full use of the slip road?

Mark one answer

- ☒ Because there is space available to reverse if you need to.
- ☒ To allow you direct access to the overtaking lanes.
- ☒ To build up a speed similar to traffic on the motorway.
- ☒ Because you can continue on the hard shoulder.

Answer

☒ **To build up a speed similar to traffic on the motorway.**

Try to join the motorway without affecting the progress of the traffic already travelling on it. At busy times this could also mean slowing down to merge into slow-moving traffic.

Question
You are joining a motorway from a slip road on the left. You should

Mark one answer

- ☒ adjust your speed to the speed of the traffic on the motorway
- ☒ accelerate as quickly as you can and ride straight out
- ☒ ride onto the hard shoulder until a gap appears
- ☒ give a left signal to join the motorway.

Answer

☒ **adjust your speed to the speed of the traffic on the motorway**

Give way to the traffic already on the motorway and join where there's a suitable gap in the traffic. Try to avoid stopping at the end of the slip road. This might not be avoidable, however, if the motorway is exceptionally busy and there isn't a clear gap in the traffic.

Question

When joining a motorway you must always

Mark one answer

- [ ] use the hard shoulder
- [ ] stop at the end of the acceleration lane
- [ ] come to a stop before joining the motorway
- [ ] give way to traffic already on the motorway.

Answer

☒ **give way to traffic already on the motorway**

The traffic may be travelling at high speed so you should adjust your speed and emerge when it's safe to do so.

Question

You are driving a car on a motorway. Unless signs show otherwise you must NOT exceed

Mark one answer

- [ ] 50 mph
- [ ] 60 mph
- [ ] 70 mph
- [ ] 80 mph.

Answer

☒ **70 mph**

The national speed limit for a car or motorcycle on the motorway is 70 mph.

Lower speed limits may be in force so look out for the signs. There might be a variable speed limit in operation to control a very busy motorway. The speed limit may change depending on the volume of traffic. There may be roadworks enforcing a low speed limit.

Question

You are riding on a motorway. Unless signs show otherwise you must NOT exceed

Mark one answer

- [ ] 50 mph
- [ ] 60 mph
- [ ] 70 mph
- [ ] 80 mph.

Answer

☒ **70 mph**

Ride in accordance with the conditions. Bad weather, heavy traffic or roadworks will limit your speed.

Question

What is the national speed limit for cars and motorcycles in the centre lane of a three-lane motorway?

Mark one answer

- [ ] 40 mph.
- [ ] 50 mph.
- [ ] 60 mph.
- [ ] 70 mph.

Answer

☒ **70 mph.**

Unless otherwise indicted the speed limit for the motorway applies to all the lanes. Be on the lookout for any indication of speed limit changes due to roadworks or traffic flow control.

Question
What is the national speed limit on motorways for cars and motorcycles?

Mark one answer
- ☒ 30 mph.
- ☒ 50 mph.
- ☒ 60 mph.
- ☒ 70 mph.

Answer
 70 mph.

Speed limits may be altered due to weather conditions. Look out for signs on the central reserve or above your lane.

Question
You are towing a trailer on a motorway. What is your maximum speed limit?

Mark one answer
- ☒ 40 mph.
- ☒ 50 mph.
- ☒ 60 mph.
- ☒ 70 mph.

Answer
 60 mph.

Don't forget that you're towing a trailer. If you're towing a small, light trailer it won't reduce your vehicle's performance by very much. Strong winds or buffeting from large vehicles might cause it to snake from side to side. Be aware of your speed and don't exceed the lower limit imposed.

Question
Which of the these IS NOT allowed to travel in the right-hand lane of a three-lane motorway?

Mark one answer
- ☒ A small delivery van.
- ☒ A motorcycle.
- ☒ A vehicle towing a trailer.
- ☒ A motorcycle and side-car.

Answer
 A vehicle towing a trailer.

A vehicle with a trailer is restricted to 60 mph. For this reason it isn't allowed in the right-hand lane as it might hold up the faster-moving traffic that wishes to overtake in that lane.

Question
On a three-lane motorway which lane should you use for normal driving?

Mark one answer
- ☒ Left.
- ☒ Right.
- ☒ Centre.
- ☒ Either the right or centre.

Answer
 Left.

On a three-lane motorway you should travel in the left-hand lane unless you're overtaking. This applies regardless of the speed you're travelling at.

Question

A basic rule when driving on motorways is

Mark one answer

☒ use the lane that has least traffic

☒ keep to the left lane unless overtaking

☒ overtake on the side that is clearest

☒ try to keep above 50 mph to prevent congestion.

Answer

☒ **keep to the left lane unless overtaking**

When you've overtaken, move back into the left-hand lane as soon as it's safe to do so. Don't cut across in front of the vehicle that you're overtaking.

Question

On a three-lane motorway why should you normally ride in the left lane?

Mark one answer

☒ The lanes on the right are for overtaking.

☒ The left lane is for motorcycles only.

☒ The left lane is only for slower vehicles.

☒ Motorcycles are not allowed in the far right lane.

Answer

☒ **The lanes on the right are for overtaking.**

Change lane only if necessary. When you do change lane observe, signal and manoeuvre in good time. Always remember your 'lifesaver' check. This is a final, quick rearward glance before you manoeuvre.

Question

You are driving on a three-lane motorway at 70 mph. There is no traffic ahead. Which lane should you use?

Mark one answer

☒ Any lane.

☒ Middle lane.

☒ Right lane.

☒ Left lane.

Answer

☒ **Left lane.**

Use the left-hand lane if it's free, regardless of the speed you're travelling at.

Question

You are driving on a motorway. You have to slow down quickly due to a hazard. You should

Mark one answer

☒ switch on your hazard lights

☒ switch on your headlights

☒ sound your horn

☒ flash your headlights.

Answer

☒ **switch on your hazard lights**

Switching these lights on will warn the traffic behind you that you're slowing quickly or stopping. Switch them off again as the queue forms behind you.

Question
The left-hand lane on a three-lane motorway is for use by

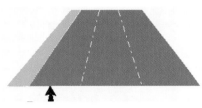

Mark one answer
- ☒ any vehicle
- ☒ large vehicles only
- ☒ emergency vehicles only
- ☒ slow vehicles only.

Answer
☒ any vehicle

On a motorway all traffic should use the left-hand lane unless overtaking. If you need to overtake use the centre or right-hand lanes.

Make sure that you move back to the left-hand lane when you've finished overtaking. Don't stay in the middle or right-hand lanes if the left-hand lane is free.

Question
The left-hand lane of a motorway should be used for

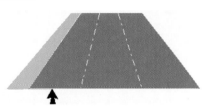

Mark one answer
- ☒ breakdowns and emergencies only
- ☒ overtaking slower traffic in the other lanes
- ☒ slow vehicles only
- ☒ normal driving.

Answer
☒ normal driving

You must be aware that large vehicles aren't allowed into the right-hand lane to overtake. Don't impede their progress by staying in the middle lane. Move back into the left-hand lane as soon as it is safe to do so.

Question
What is the right hand-lane used for on a three-lane motorway?

Mark one answer
- ☒ Emergency vehicles only.
- ☒ Overtaking.
- ☒ Vehicles towing trailers.
- ☒ Coaches only.

Answer
☒ Overtaking.

You should keep to the left and only use the right-hand lane if you're passing slower-moving traffic.

Question

For what reason may you use the right-hand lane of a motorway?

Mark one answer

☒ For keeping out of the way of lorries.

☒ For driving at more than 70 mph.

☒ For turning right.

☒ For overtaking other vehicles.

Answer

☒ **For overtaking other vehicles.**

The right-hand lanes of the motorway are for overtaking. Sometimes you may be directed into a right-hand lane as a result of roadworks or an accident. Be guided by the signs or police directing the traffic.

Question

On motorways you should never overtake on the left UNLESS

Mark one answer

☒ you can see well ahead that the hard shoulder is clear

☒ the traffic in the right-hand lane is signalling right

☒ you warn drivers behind by signalling left

☒ there is a queue of traffic to your right that is moving more slowly.

Answer

☒ **there is a queue of traffic to your right that is moving more slowly**

Only overtake on the left if traffic is moving slowly in queues and the traffic on the right is moving slower.

Question

On a motorway you may ONLY stop on the hard shoulder

Mark one answer

☒ in an emergency

☒ if you feel tired and need to rest

☒ if you accidentally go past the exit that you wanted to take

☒ to pick up a hitchhiker.

Answer

☒ **in an emergency**

Don't stop on the hard shoulder to

- have a rest or a picnic
- pick up hitchhikers
- answer a mobile phone
- check a road map.

Never reverse along the hard shoulder if you accidentally go past the exit you wanted.

Question

You are driving on a motorway. The car ahead shows its hazard lights for a short time. This tells you that

Mark one answer

- [ ] the driver wants you to overtake
- [ ] the other car is going to change lanes
- [ ] traffic ahead is slowing or stopping suddenly
- [ ] there is a police speed check up ahead.

Answer

 traffic ahead is slowing or stopping suddenly

There may be an accident or queuing due to roadworks. Look well ahead, not just at the car in front, and you'll get an earlier warning of any hazard.

Question

You are driving on a motorway. You have to slow down quickly due to a hazard. You should

Mark one answer

- [ ] switch on your headlights
- [ ] switch on your hazard lights
- [ ] sound your horn
- [ ] flash your headlights.

Answer

 switch on your hazard lights

The traffic behind you will be given an extra warning, in addition to your brake lights. Switch them off again as the queue forms behind you.

Question

Which vehicles are normally fitted with amber flashing beacons on the roof?

Mark two answers

- [ ] Doctor's car.
- [ ] Bomb disposal team.
- [ ] Blood transfusion team.
- [ ] Breakdown recovery vehicles.
- [ ] Coastguard.
- [ ] Maintenance vehicles.

Answers

 Breakdown recovery vehicles.

Maintenance vehicles.

These vehicles are often carrying out tasks on the hard shoulder. If you see a yellow beacon ahead, be prepared in case you have to give them more room by moving into the middle lane.

Question

You get a puncture on the motorway. You manage to get your vehicle onto the hard shoulder. You should

Mark one answer

☒ change the wheel yourself immediately

☒ use the emergency telephone and call for assistance

☒ try to wave down another vehicle for help

☒ only change the wheel if you have a passenger to help you.

Answer

☒ **use the emergency telephone and call for assistance**

Due to the danger from passing traffic you shouldn't attempt repairs on the hard shoulder, especially if you have to change an offside wheel.

Question

How should you use the emergency telephone on a motorway?

Mark one answer

☒ Stay close to the carriageway.

☒ Face the oncoming traffic.

☒ Keep your back to the traffic.

☒ Keep your head in the kiosk.

Answer

☒ **Face the oncoming traffic.**

Traffic is passing you at speed. The draught from a large lorry could unsteady you, so be prepared. By facing the oncoming traffic you can spot this in advance, as well as other hazards approaching.

Question

What should you use the hard shoulder of a motorway for?

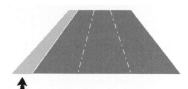

Mark one answer

☒ Stopping in an emergency.

☒ Overtaking.

☒ Stopping when you are tired.

☒ Joining the motorway.

Answer

☒ **Stopping in an emergency.**

Don't use the hard shoulder for stopping other than for emergencies. Drive to the next exit or service station if you're able to do so safely.

Question

After a breakdown you need to rejoin the main carriageway of a motorway from the hard shoulder. You should

Mark one answer

 move out onto the carriageway then build up your speed

 move out onto the carriageway using your hazard lights

 gain speed on the hard shoulder before moving out onto the carriageway

 wait on the hard shoulder until someone flashes their headlights at you.

Answer

 gain speed on the hard shoulder before moving out onto the carriageway

Wait for a safe gap in the traffic before you move out. Indicate your intention but don't force your way into the traffic.

Question

Your vehicle has broken down on a motorway. You are not able to stop on the hard shoulder. What should you do FIRST?

Mark one answer

 Switch on your hazard warning lights.

 Stop following traffic and ask for help.

 Attempt to repair your vehicle quickly.

 Place a warning triangle in the road.

Answer

 Switch on your hazard warning lights.

Use your hazard warning lights to warn others.

DON'T TRY TO REPAIR THE VEHICLE.

Question

You are travelling in the left-hand lane of a busy motorway. Signs indicate that your lane is closed 800 yards ahead. You should

Mark one answer

 signal right, then pull up and wait for someone to give way

 switch on your hazard warning lights and edge over to the lane on your right

 wait until you reach the obstruction, then move across to the right

 move over to the lane on your right as soon as it is safe to do so.

Answer

 move over to the lane on your right as soon as it is safe to do so

Always look well ahead and be aware of road signs. If you see that your lane will be closing move across to the next lane in good time. The road signs will have given plenty of warning. Don't

- wait until the last moment before trying to change lane
- expect someone to let you in
- stop.

Be aware that the traffic on the right may be moving very quickly.

Question

When may you stop on a motorway?

Mark three answers

☒ If you have to read a map.

☒ When you are tired and need a rest.

☒ If red lights show above your lane.

☒ When told to by the police.

☒ If a child in the car feels ill.

☒ In an emergency or a breakdown.

Answers

☒ **If red lights show above your lane.**

☒ **When told to by the police.**

☒ **In an emergency or a breakdown.**

You may only stop on the carriageway of a motorway

- when told to do so by the police
- when flashing red lights show above the lane that you're in
- in a traffic jam
- in an emergency or breakdown.

Question

You are driving on a motorway. There are red flashing lights above your lane. You must

Mark one answer

☒ pull onto the hard shoulder

☒ slow down and watch for further signals

☒ leave at the next exit

☒ stop and wait.

Answer

☒ **stop and wait**

Flashing red lights above every lane mean you must not go on any further. You'll also see a red cross illuminated. Stop and wait. Don't

- change lanes
- continue
- pull onto the hard shoulder (unless in an emergency).

Question

The minimum safe time gap to keep between you and the vehicle in front in good conditions is at least

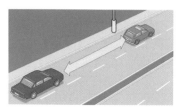

Mark one answer

☒ four seconds

☒ one second

☒ three seconds

☒ two seconds.

Answer

☒ **two seconds**

Driving too close to the vehicle in front can cause accidents, potentially involving many vehicles and causing serious injury. As you drive at higher speeds you must increase your separation distance from the car in front. One way to judge this is to use the 'Two-Second Rule.'

Pick an object some distance ahead, such as a lamp-post or a bridge. As the vehicle in front passes it begin to say

'Only a fool breaks the Two-Second Rule.'

If you pass the object before you finish saying it, you're too close. Drop back and try again.

Question

When driving through a contraflow system on a motorway you should

Mark one answer

- ☒ ensure that you do not exceed 30 mph, for safety
- ☒ keep a good distance from the vehicle ahead, for safety
- ☒ switch lanes to keep the traffic flowing
- ☒ drive close to the vehicle ahead to reduce queues.

Answer

☒ **keep a good distance from the vehicle ahead, for safety**

There's likely to be a speed restriction in force. Keep to this. Don't

- switch lanes
- drive too close to other traffic.

There will be no permanent barrier between you and the traffic coming towards you. Be extra cautious.

Question

You are intending to leave the motorway at the next exit. Before you reach the exit you should normally position your vehicle

Mark one answer

- ☒ in the middle lane
- ☒ in the left-hand lane
- ☒ on the hard shoulder
- ☒ in any lane.

Answer

☒ **in the left hand lane**

You'll see the first sign one mile from the exit. If you're travelling at 60 miles an hour in the right hand-lane you'll only have about 50 seconds before you reach the countdown markers. There's another sign at the half-mile point. Think about what you need to do to be in the left-hand lane in good time. Don't cut across traffic at the last moment.

Question

What do these motorway signs show?

Mark one answer

- ☒ They are countdown markers to a bridge.
- ☒ They are distance markers to the next telephone.
- ☒ They are countdown markers to the next exit.
- ☒ They warn of a police control ahead.

Answer

☒ **They are countdown markers to the next exit.**

The exit from a motorway is indicated by countdown markers. These are positioned 100 yards apart, the first being 300 yards from the slip road. Try to get yourself into the left lane in good time.

Question

At night, when leaving a well-lit motorway service area, you should

Mark one answer

- ☒ drive for some time using only your sidelights
- ☒ give your eyes time to adjust to the darkness
- ☒ switch on your interior light until your eyes adjust
- ☒ close your eyes for a moment before leaving the slip road.

Answer

- ☒ **give your eyes time to adjust to the darkness**

You should have your eyesight checked regularly. If you can't see well at night it could be that your eyes are to blame. Night driving might show a need for a check with an optician.

Question

You are driving on a motorway. By mistake, you go past the exit that you wanted to take. You should

Mark one answer

- ☒ carefully reverse on the hard shoulder
- ☒ carry on to the next exit
- ☒ carefully reverse in the left-hand lane
- ☒ make a U-turn at the next gap in the central reservation.

Answer

- ☒ **carry on to the next exit**

Don't

- reverse anywhere
- make a U-turn.

This is highly dangerous, as high-speed traffic might not be able to take evasive action.

Question

On a motorway the reflective amber studs can be found between

Mark one answer

- ☒ the hard shoulder and the carriageway
- ☒ the acceleration lane and the carriageway
- ☒ the central reservation and the carriageway
- ☒ each pair of the lanes.

Answer

- ☒ **the central reservation and the carriageway**

On motorways reflective studs are fitted into the road to help you

- in the dark
- in conditions of poor visibility.

The reflective studs are coloured. These will help you to know which lane you're in and where slip roads join or leave the motorway.

Question
You are driving on a three-lane motorway. There are red reflective studs on your left and white ones to your right. Where are you?

Mark one answer

☒ In the right-hand lane.

☒ In the middle lane.

☒ On the hard shoulder.

☒ In the left-hand lane.

Answer

☒ **In the left-hand lane.**

The colours of the reflective studs on the motorway and their locations are

Red
- between the hard shoulder and the carriageway.

White
- lane markings.

Amber
- between the edge of the carriageway and the central reserve.

Green
- along slip road exits and entrances.

Bright Green/Yellow
- roadworks and contraflow systems.

Question
What colour are the reflective studs between a motorway and its slip road?

Mark one answer

☒ Amber.

☒ White.

☒ Green.

☒ Red.

Answer

☒ **Green.**

These will help you when driving in conditions of poor visibility or in the dark.

Question
You are travelling on a motorway. What colour are the reflective studs on the left of the carriageway?

Mark one answer

☒ Green.

☒ Red.

☒ White.

☒ Amber.

Answer

☒ **Red.**

When you have passed your practical test ask your Approved Driving Instructor (ADI) about lessons on the motorway. Good professional instruction will help you to become confident and safe on the motorway.

This section looks at rules of the road.

The questions will ask you about

- speed limits
- lane discipline
- parking
- lighting.

Question
What is the meaning of this sign?

Mark one answer

- ☒ Local speed limit applies.
- ☒ No waiting on the carriageway.
- ☒ National speed limit applies.
- ☒ No entry to vehicular traffic.

Answer

☒ **National speed limit applies.**

This sign doesn't tell you the speed limit in figures. You should know the speed limit for the type of road that you're on. Study *The Highway Code*.

Question
What is the national speed limit for cars and motorcycles on a dual carriageway?

Mark one answer

- ☒ 30 mph.
- ☒ 50 mph.
- ☒ 60 mph.
- ☒ 70 mph.

Answer

☒ **70 mph.**

Ensure that you know the speed limit for the road that you're driving on.

The speed limit on a dual carriageway or motorway is 70 mph for cars and motorcycles, unless there are signs to indicate otherwise.

The speed limits for different vehicles are listed in *The Highway Code*.

Question
A single carriageway road has this sign. What's the maximum permitted speed for a car towing a trailer?

Mark one answer

- ☒ 30 mph.
- ☒ 40 mph.
- ☒ 50 mph.
- ☒ 60 mph.

Answer

☒ **50 mph.**

When towing trailers, speed limits are also lower on dual carriageways and motorways. On these roads vehicles towing a trailer are restricted to 60 mph.

Question

What is the national speed limit on a single carriageway road for cars and motorcycles?

Mark one answer

☒ 70 mph.

☒ 60 mph.

☒ 50 mph.

☒ 30 mph.

Answer

☒ **60 mph.**

Exceeding the speed limit is dangerous and can result in you receiving penalty points on your licence. It isn't worth it. Know the speed limit of the road that you're driving on by observing the road signs.

Question

You are driving along a road that has no traffic signs. There are street lights. What is the speed limit?

Mark one answer

☒ 20 mph.

☒ 30 mph.

☒ 40 mph.

☒ 60 mph.

Answer

☒ **30 mph.**

If you aren't sure of the speed limit it can be indicated by the presence of street lights. If there is street lighting the speed limit will be 30 mph unless otherwise indicated.

Question

There are no speed limit signs on the road. How is a 30 mph limit indicated?

Mark one answer

☒ By hazard warning lines.

☒ By street lighting.

☒ By pedestrian islands.

☒ By double or single yellow lines.

Answer

☒ **By street lighting.**

This usually indicates a 30 mph speed limit when there are no other signs to show other limits.

Question

Where you see street lights but no speed limit signs the limit is usually

Mark one answer

☒ 30 mph.

☒ 40 mph.

☒ 50 mph.

☒ 60 mph.

Answer

☒ **30 mph.**

Question
You see this sign ahead of you. It means

Mark one answer

☒ start to slow down to 30 mph after passing it

☒ you are leaving the 30 mph speed limit area

☒ do not exceed 30 mph after passing it

☒ the minimum speed limit ahead is 30 mph.

Answer

☒ **do not exceed 30 mph after passing it**

Adjust your speed in good time. Don't

- brake sharply
- wait until you're beyond the limit sign before slowing down.

Question
If you see a 30 mph limit ahead it means

Mark one answer

☒ that the restriction applies only during the working day

☒ that you must not exceed this speed

☒ that it is a guide and you are allowed to drive 10% faster

☒ that you must keep your speed up to 30 mph.

Answer

☒ **that you must not exceed this speed**

Because the sign is round it gives you an order. You must obey it.

In a built-up area there are many hazards that call for reduced speed, such as

- pedestrians
- cyclists
- junctions
- busy traffic situations.

Question
What does a speed limit sign like this mean?

Mark one answer

- ☒ It is safe to drive at the speed shown.
- ☒ The speed shown is the advised maximum.
- ☒ The speed shown allows for various road and weather conditions.
- ☒ You must not exceed the speed shown.

Answer

❌ **You must not exceed the speed shown.**

Speed limit signs are there for a reason. There may be a large number of side roads. The lower speed limit makes emerging from these safer.

Question
You are towing a small caravan on a dual carriageway. You must not exceed

Mark one answer

- ☒ 50 mph
- ☒ 40 mph
- ☒ 70 mph
- ☒ 60 mph.

Answer

❌ **60 mph**

Due to the increased weight and width of the combined vehicles you should plan well ahead. Be extra careful in wet or windy weather. Strong winds might cause the caravan to snake from side to side. The speed limit is reduced for vehicles towing trailers to lessen the risk of this.

Question
What does this sign mean?

Mark one answer

- ☒ Minimum speed 30 mph.
- ☒ End of maximum speed.
- ☒ End of minimum speed.
- ☒ Maximum speed 30 mph.

Answer

❌ **End of minimum speed.**

A red slash through this sign indicates that the restriction has ended.

Question

You are driving along a street with parked vehicles on the left-hand side. For which THREE reasons must you keep your speed down?

Mark three answers

- [ ] So that oncoming traffic can see you more clearly.
- [ ] You may set off car alarms.
- [ ] Vehicles may be pulling out.
- [ ] Drivers' doors may open.
- [ ] Children may run out from between the vehicles.

Answers

- [x] **Vehicles may be pulling out.**
- [x] **Drivers' doors may open.**
- [x] **Children may run out from between the vehicles.**

Care must be taken where there are parked vehicles in a built-up area. Beware of

- vehicles pulling out, especially motor-cycles that are small and difficult to see
- pedestrians, especially children, who may run out from between cars
- drivers opening vehicle doors.

Question

You meet an obstruction on your side of the road. You must

Mark one answer

- [ ] drive on: it is your right of way
- [ ] give way to oncoming traffic
- [ ] wave oncoming vehicles through
- [ ] accelerate to get past first.

Answer

- [x] **give way to oncoming traffic**

If you have to pass a parked vehicle on your side of the road take care. Give way to oncoming traffic if there isn't enough room for you both to continue safely.

Question

There is a tractor ahead of you. You wish to overtake but you are NOT sure if it is safe to do so. You should

Mark one answer

- [ ] follow another overtaking vehicle through
- [ ] sound your horn to the slow vehicle to pull over
- [ ] speed through but flash your lights to oncoming traffic
- [ ] not overtake if you are in doubt.

Answer

- [x] **not overtake if you are in doubt**

Always ask yourself if you really need to overtake. Can you see well down the road? If the answer is no, don't go.

Question

You are leaving your vehicle parked on a road. When may you leave the engine running?

Mark one answer

☒ If you will be parked for less than five minutes.

☒ If the battery is flat.

☒ If there is a passenger in the vehicle.

☒ Not on any occasion.

Question

In which FOUR places must you NOT park or wait?

Mark four answers

☒ On a dual carriageway.

☒ At a bus stop.

☒ On the slope of a hill.

☒ Opposite a traffic island.

☒ In front of someone else's drive.

☒ On the brow of a hill.

Question

What is the nearest you may park your vehicle to a junction?

Mark one answer

☒ 10 metres (33 feet).

☒ 12 metres (40 feet).

☒ 15 metres (50 feet).

☒ 20 metres (65 feet).

Answer

☒ **Not on any occasion.**

When you leave your vehicle parked on a road

- switch off the engine
- make sure that there aren't any valuables visible
- shut all the windows
- lock the vehicle. Use an anti-theft device if you have one.

Answers

☒ **At a bus stop.**

☒ **Opposite a traffic island.**

☒ **In front of someone else's drive.**

☒ **On the brow of a hill.**

Care and thought should be taken when parking your own vehicle. Don't park

- on a footpath, pavement or cycle track
- near a school entrance
- on the approach to a zebra crossing (except in an authorised parking place)
- opposite another parked vehicle.

Answer

☒ **10 metres (33 feet).**

Don't park within 10 metres (33 feet) of a junction (unless in an authorized parking place) or

- where you would force other traffic to enter a tram lane
- where the kerb has been lowered to help wheelchair users
- in front of an entrance to a property
- where your vehicle might obstruct a tram.

Question

In which TWO places must you NOT park?

Mark two answers

- ☒ Near a school entrance.
- ☒ Near a police station.
- ☒ In a side road.
- ☒ At a bus stop.
- ☒ In a one-way street.

Answers

- ☒ **Near a school entrance.**
- ☒ **At a bus stop.**

It may be tempting to park where you shouldn't while you run a quick errand. Careless parking is a selfish act and could endanger other road users.

Question

In which THREE places must you NEVER park your vehicle?

Mark three answers

- ☒ Near the brow of a hill.
- ☒ At or near a bus stop.
- ☒ Where there is no pavement.
- ☒ Within 10 metres (33 feet) of a junction.
- ☒ On a 40 mph road.

Answers

- ☒ **Near the brow of a hill.**
- ☒ **At or near a bus stop.**
- ☒ **Within 10 metres (33 feet) of a junction.**

Other traffic will have to pull out to pass you. This might mean they have to use the other side of the road where there might be oncoming traffic.

Parking near a junction could restrict the view for emerging vehicles.

Question

You want to park and you see this sign. On the days and times shown you should

Meter
ZONE

Mon - Fri
8.30 am - 6.30 pm
Saturday
8.30 am - 1.30 pm

Mark one answer

- ☒ park in a bay and not pay
- ☒ park on yellow lines and pay
- ☒ park on yellow lines and not pay
- ☒ park in a bay and pay

Answer

- ☒ **park in a bay and pay**

Parking restrictions vary from town to town. Look at the signs carefully. Parking in the wrong place could cause an obstruction and you could be fined.

Question
What is the meaning of this sign?

Mark one answer

 No entry.

 Waiting restrictions.

 National speed limit.

 School crossing patrol.

Answer
 Waiting restrictions.

Don't cause an obstruction by stopping or waiting where there are restrictions

You should know the meaning of road signs. Buy a copy of *Know Your Traffic Signs* and study it.

Question
At which of these places are you **sometimes** allowed to park your vehicle?

Mark one answer

 On the nearside lane of a motorway.

 On a clearway.

 Where there is a single broken yellow line.

 On the zigzag lines of a zebra crossing.

Answer
 Where there is a single broken yellow line.

You may be able to park where there are broken lines along the edge of the road. Check the signs at the side of the road for parking restrictions. Where there are double yellow lines you may not be able to park at all.

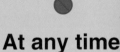

Question
What MUST you have to park in a disabled space?

Mark one answer

 An orange badge.

 A wheelchair.

 An advanced driver certificate.

 A modified vehicle.

Answer
 An orange badge.

Don't park in a space reserved for disabled people unless you or your passenger are a disabled badge-holder. The badge must be displayed on your vehicle in the bottom left-hand corner of the windscreen.

Question

You are looking for somewhere to park your vehicle. The area is full EXCEPT for spaces marked 'disabled use'. You must

Mark one answer

☒ use these spaces when elsewhere is full

☒ stay with your vehicle when you park there

☒ use these spaces, disabled or not

☒ not park there unless permitted.

Question

Your vehicle is parked on the road at night. When must you use sidelights?

Mark one answer

☒ Where there are continuous white lines in the middle of the road.

☒ Where the speed limit exceeds 30 mph.

☒ Where you are facing oncoming traffic.

☒ Where you are near a bus stop.

Question

You park overnight on a road with a 40 mph speed limit. You should

Mark one answer

☒ park facing the traffic

☒ park with sidelights on

☒ park with dipped headlights on

☒ park near a street light.

Answer

✖ not park there unless permitted

Don't be selfish. Find somewhere else to park even if it means that you have to walk further. Leave the space free for those who can't do this.

Answer

 ✖ Where the speed limit exceeds 30 mph.

When parking at night, park in the direction of the traffic. This will enable other road users to see the reflectors on the rear of your vehicle.

Use your sidelights if the speed limit is over 30 mph or you're parking a vehicle over 1,525 kg.

Answer

 ✖ park with sidelights on

Make sure that other road users can see your vehicle. Park in the direction of the traffic flow so that your vehicle isn't mistaken for a moving oncoming car.

Question

You can park on the right-hand side of a road at night

Mark one answer

☒ in a one-way street

☒ with your sidelights on

☒ more than 10 metres (33 feet) from a junction

☒ under a lamp-post.

Answer

☒ **in a one way street**

Vehicles are fitted with red rear reflectors that show up when headlights shine on them. These are useful when cars are parked at night but will only reflect if the vehicles are parked in the same direction as the traffic passing alongside. Normally you should park on the left, but if you're in a one-way street the right-hand side is OK too.

Question

On a three-lane dual carriageway the right-hand lane can be used for

Mark one answer

☒ overtaking only, never turning right

☒ overtaking or turning right

☒ fast-moving traffic only

☒ turning right only, never overtaking.

Answer

☒ **overtaking or turning right**

Use the left-hand lane at other times. When overtaking on a dual carriageway be on the lookout for vehicles ahead that are turning right. They're likely to be slowing or stopped. You need to see them in good time so that you can take appropriate action.

Question

You are driving at night with full beam headlights on. A vehicle is overtaking you. You should dip your lights

Mark one answer

☒ some time after the vehicle has passed you

☒ before the vehicle starts to pass you

☒ only if the other driver dips his headlights

☒ as soon as the vehicle passes you.

Answer

☒ **as soon as the vehicle passes you**

Your lights on full beam could dazzle the driver in front. Make sure that your light beam falls short of the vehicle in front.

Question

You are driving on a two-lane dual carriageway. For which TWO of the following would you use the right-hand lane?

Mark two answers

☒ Turning right.

☒ Normal driving.

☒ Driving at the minimum allowed speed.

☒ Constant high-speed driving.

☒ Overtaking slower traffic.

☒ Mending punctures.

Answers

☒ **Turning right.**

☒ **Overtaking slower traffic.**

If you overtake on a dual carriageway move back into the left lane as soon as it's safe. Don't cut in across the path of the vehicle you've just passed.

Question

You are driving in the right lane of a dual carriageway. You see signs showing that the right lane is closed 800 yards ahead. You should

GET IN LANE

800 yards

Mark one answer

☒ keep in that lane until you reach the queue.

☒ move to the left immediately.

☒ wait and see which lane is moving faster.

☒ move to the left in good time.

Answer

☒ **move to the left in good time**

Keep a lookout for traffic signs. If you're directed to change lanes do so in good time. Don't

• push your way into traffic in another lane

• leave changing lanes until the last moment.

Question

You are entering an area of roadworks. There is a temporary speed limit displayed. You must

Mark one answer

☒ not exceed the speed limit

☒ obey the limit only during rush hour

☒ accept the speed limit as advisable

☒ obey the limit except for overnight.

Answer

☒ **not exceed the speed limit**

Where there are extra hazards, such as roadworks it's often necessary to slow traffic down by imposing a temporary speed limit. These speed limits aren't advisory – they must be adhered to.

Question
While driving, you approach roadworks. You see a temporary maximum speed limit sign. You must

Mark one answer

☒ comply with the sign during the working day

☒ comply with the sign at all times

☒ comply with the sign when the lanes are narrow

☒ comply with the sign during the hours of darkness.

Answer

❌ **comply with the sign at all times**

The sign has been put there to allow traffic to deal with the hazard at a low speed. Reduce the risk and don't exceed the limit.

Question
You may drive a motor car in this bus lane

Mark one answer

☒ outside its operation hours

☒ to get to the front of a traffic queue

☒ at no times at all

☒ to overtake slow moving traffic.

Answer

❌ **outside its operation hours**

Make full use of bus lanes if it's permitted. This can often be at times other than rush hours. Check the sign. Times will differ from place to place.

Question
As a car driver which THREE lanes must you NOT use?

Mark three answers

☒ Crawler lane.

☒ Bus lane at the times shown.

☒ Overtaking lane.

☒ Acceleration lane.

☒ Cycle lane.

☒ Tram lane.

Answers

❌ **Bus lane at the times shown.**

❌ **Cycle lane.**

❌ **Tram lane.**

Look out for signs or road markings that tell you which lane to use. Some lanes can only be used by certain road users. These might be to allow the traffic to flow, or to protect vulnerable road users.

Question

You are driving on a road that has a cycle lane. The lane is marked by a solid white line. This means that

Mark two answers

☒ you must not drive in the lane unless it is unavoidable

☒ the lane cannot be used for parking your vehicle

☒ you can drive in the lane at any time

☒ the lane must be used by motorcyclists in heavy traffic.

Answers

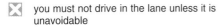 **you must not drive in the lane unless it is unavoidable**

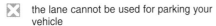 **the lane cannot be used for parking your vehicle**

Where sign or road markings show lanes are for cyclists only, leave them free.

Question

As a motorcycle rider which TWO lanes must you NOT use?

Mark two answers

☒ Crawler lane.

☒ Overtaking lane.

☒ Acceleration lane.

☒ Cycle lane.

☒ Tram lane.

Answers

☒ **Cycle lane.**

☒ **Tram lane.**

In some towns motorcycles are permitted to use bus lanes. Check the signs carefully.

Question

You are approaching a busy junction. There are several lanes with road markings. At the last moment you realise that you are in the wrong lane. You should

Mark one answer

☒ continue in that lane

☒ force your way across

☒ stop until the area has cleared

☒ use clear arm signals to cut across.

Answer

☒ **continue in that lane**

There are times where road markings can be obscured by queueing traffic, or you might be unsure of your correct lane. Don't cut across lanes or bully other drivers to let you in. Follow the lane you're in and find somewhere safe to turn around if you need to.

Question

Where may you overtake on a one-way street?

Mark one answer

☒ Only on the left-hand side.

☒ Overtaking is not allowed.

☒ Only on the right-hand side.

☒ Either on the right or the left.

Question

You are going along a single-track road with passing places only on the right. The driver behind wishes to overtake. You should

Mark one answer

☒ speed up to get away from the following driver

☒ switch on your hazard warning lights

☒ wait opposite a passing place on your right

☒ drive into a passing place on your right.

Question

You are on a road that is only wide enough for one vehicle. There is a car coming towards you. Which TWO of these would be correct?

Mark two answers

☒ Pull into a passing place on your right.

☒ Force the other driver to reverse.

☒ Pull into a passing place if your vehicle is wider.

☒ Pull into a passing place on your left.

☒ Wait opposite a passing place on your right.

☒ Wait opposite a passing place on your left.

Answer

✖ Either on the right or the left.

You can overtake other traffic on either side when travelling in a one-way street. Make full use of your mirrors and ensure that it's clear all around before you attempt to overtake. Look for signs and road markings and use the most suitable lane for your destination.

Answer

✖ wait opposite a passing place on your right

Some roads are only wide enough for one vehicle. Often this type of road has special passing places where the road is widened for a short distance.

If there's a car coming toward you pull into a passing place on your left or stop opposite one on your right. Don't

• force other vehicles to reverse

• pull into the passing place on the right.

Answers

✖ Pull into a passing place on your left.

✖ Wait opposite a passing place on your right.

If you meet another vehicle in a narrow road and the passing place is on the right, pull up opposite it. This will allow the oncoming vehicle to pull into it and pass you safely.

Question

Signals are normally given by direction indicators and

Mark one answer

☒ brake lights

☒ side lights

☒ fog lights

☒ interior lights.

Answer

☒ **brake lights**

Your brake lights will give an indication to traffic behind that you're slowing down. Good anticipation will allow you time to check your mirrors before slowing.

If you're intending to change direction you should use your direction indicators before you brake.

Question

When going straight ahead at a roundabout you should

Mark one answer

☒ indicate left before leaving the roundabout

☒ not indicate at any time

☒ indicate right when approaching the roundabout

☒ indicate left when approaching the roundabout.

Answer

☒ **indicate left before leaving the roundabout**

When you want to go ahead at a roundabout indicate left just after you pass the exit before the one you wish to take. Don't

- signal right on approach
- signal left on approach.

Question

Which vehicle might have to use a different course to normal at roundabouts?

Mark one answer

☒ Sports car.

☒ Van.

☒ Estate car.

☒ Long vehicle.

Answer

☒ **Long vehicle.**

A long vehicle may have to straddle lanes either on or approaching a roundabout so that the rear wheels don't cut in over the kerb. Stay well back and give it room.

Question

You are going straight ahead at a roundabout. How should you signal?

Mark one answer

☒ Signal right on the approach and then left to leave the roundabout.

☒ Signal left as you leave the roundabout.

☒ Signal left on the approach to the roundabout and keep the signal on until you leave.

☒ Signal left just after you pass the exit before the one you'll take.

Answer

 Signal left just after you pass the exit before the one you will take.

To go straight ahead at a roundabout you should normally approach in the left-hand lane. Where there are road markings, use the lane indicated.

Ensure that you signal correctly and in good time. Other road users need to know your intentions.

Question

You are turning right at a large roundabout. Just before you leave the roundabout you should

Mark one answer

☒ take a 'lifesaver' glance over your left shoulder.

☒ take a 'lifesaver' glance over your right shoulder.

☒ put on your right indicator.

☒ cancel the left indicator.

Answer

☒ **take a 'lifesaver' glance over your left shoulder**

You must be aware of what's happening behind and alongside you. A final, quick rearward glance will give you the chance to react if it isn't safe to make the manoeuvre.

Question

You may make a U-turn

Mark one answer

☒ when it is safe on a wide road

☒ on a motorway, when it is safe

☒ in a wide one-way street

☒ by mounting both pavements carefully.

Answer

☒ **when it is safe on a wide road**

This manoeuvre should only be used when there's no traffic approaching in either direction. Make sure that you have the time and space to complete it.

Question

At a crossroads there are no signs or road markings. Two vehicles approach. Which has priority?

Mark one answer

☒ Neither vehicle.

☒ The vehicle travelling the fastest.

☒ The vehicle on the widest road.

☒ Vehicles approaching from the right.

Answer

 Neither vehicle.

At a crossroads where there are no 'give way' signs or road markings BE VERY CAREFUL. No vehicle has priority, even if the size of the roads are different.

Question
At a crossroads with no road markings who has priority?

Mark one answer

☒ Traffic from the left.
☒ Traffic from the right.
☒ Nobody.
☒ Traffic from ahead.

Question
Who has priority at an unmarked crossroads?

Mark one answer

☒ The driver of the larger vehicle.
☒ No one.
☒ The driver who is going faster.
☒ The driver on the wider road.

Answer
☒ **Nobody.**

Never assume that you have priority at a junction where there are no road signs or markings. This applies even in spite of the size of the road you're emerging from. Respond in a safe and responsible manner. Anticipate and adjust your speed – don't take risks.

Answer
☒ **No one.**

Practise good observation in all directions before you emerge or make a turn.

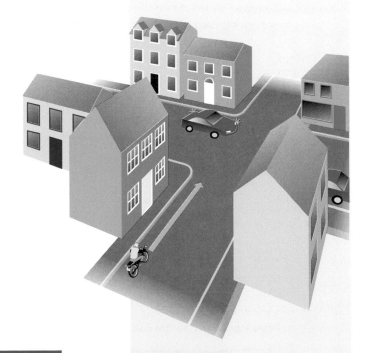

Question

You are intending to turn right at a junction. An oncoming driver is also turning right. It will normally be safer to

Mark one answer

- [x] keep the other vehicle to your RIGHT and turn behind it (offside to offside)
- [x] keep the other vehicle to your LEFT and turn in front of it (nearside to nearside)
- [x] carry on and turn at the next junction instead
- [x] hold back and wait for the other driver to turn first.

Answer

- [x] **keep the other vehicle to your RIGHT and turn behind it (offside to offside)**

At some junctions the layout may make it difficult to turn this way. Be prepared to pass nearside to nearside, but take extra care. Your view ahead will be obscured by the vehicle turning in front of you.

Question

While driving, you intend to turn left into a minor road. On the approach you should

Mark one answer

- [x] keep just left of the middle of the road
- [x] keep in the middle of the road
- [x] swing out wide just before turning
- [x] keep well to the left of the road.

Answer

- [x] **keep well to the left of the road**

Don't swing out into the centre of the road in order to make the turn. This could endanger oncoming traffic and mislead other road users of your intentions.

Question

You may only enter a box junction when

Mark one answer

- [x] there are less than two vehicles in front of you
- [x] the traffic lights show green
- [x] your exit road is clear
- [x] you need to turn left.

Answer

- [x] **your exit road is clear**

Box junctions are marked on the road to prevent the road becoming blocked.

Don't enter the box unless your exit road is clear. You may only wait in the box if your exit road is clear but oncoming traffic is preventing you from completing the turn.

Question
You may wait in a yellow box junction when

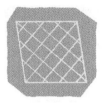

Answer

☒ **oncoming traffic is preventing you from turning right**

The purpose of this road marking is to keep the centre of the junction clear of queuing traffic when the lights change priority. Don't stop in it if you aren't turning right.

Mark one answer

☒ oncoming traffic is preventing you from turning right

☒ you are in a queue of traffic turning left

☒ you are in a queue of traffic to go ahead

☒ you are on a roundabout.

Question
You want to turn right at a box junction. You should

Mark one answer

☒ wait in the box junction if your exit is clear

☒ wait before the junction until it is clear of all traffic

☒ drive on: you cannot turn right at box junction

☒ drive slowly into the box junction when signalled by oncoming traffic.

Answer

☒ **wait in the box junction if your exit is clear**

As the lights change priority the oncoming traffic will stop, allowing you to proceed.

Question
On which THREE occasions MUST you stop your vehicle?

Mark three answers

☒ When involved in an accident.

☒ At a red traffic light.

☒ When signalled to do so by a police officer.

☒ At a junction with double broken white lines.

☒ At a pelican crossing when the amber light is flashing and no pedestrians are crossing.

Answers

☒ **When involved in an accident.**

☒ **At a red traffic light.**

☒ **When signalled to do so by a police officer.**

Don't stop or hold up traffic unnecessarily. However you MUST stop when signalled to do so by

- a police officer
- a school crossing patrol
- a red traffic light

or when you have had an accident.

Question

You MUST stop when signalled to do so by which THREE of these?

Mark three answers

- [x] A police officer.
- [x] A pedestrian.
- [x] A school crossing patrol.
- [x] A bus driver.
- [x] A red traffic light.

Answers

- [x] **A police officer.**
- [x] **A school crossing patrol.**
- [x] **A red traffic light.**

Looking well ahead and 'reading' the road will help you to anticipate hazards. This will allow you to stop safely if asked to do so by a person or a road sign.

Question

You are waiting at a level crossing. The red warning lights continue to flash after a train has passed by. What should you do?

Mark one answer

- [x] Get out and investigate.
- [x] Telephone the signal operator.
- [x] Continue to wait.
- [x] Drive across carefully.

Answer

- [x] **Continue to wait.**

At a level crossing flashing red lights mean you should stop. If the train passes but the lights keep flashing, wait. There may be another train coming.

Question

You are driving over a level crossing. The warning lights come on and a bell rings. What should you do?

Mark one answer

- [x] Get everyone out of the vehicle immediately.
- [x] Stop and reverse back to clear the crossing.
- [x] Keep going and clear the crossing.
- [x] Stop immediately and use your hazard warning lights.

Answer

- [x] **Keep going and clear the crossing.**

Keep going – don't stop on the crossing. If the warning lights come on as you're approaching the crossing, stop. Don't try to dart across before the train comes.

Question

You will see these markers when approaching

Mark one answer

- [x] a concealed level crossing
- [x] the end of a motorway
- [x] a concealed 'road narrows' sign
- [x] the end of a dual carriageway.

Answer

 a concealed level crossing

There may be a bend before a level crossing, in which case you won't be able to see barriers or waiting traffic ahead. These signs give you an early warning that you may find these hazards just around the bend.

Question

You are waiting at a level crossing. A train has passed but the lights keep flashing. You must

Mark one answer

- [x] carry on waiting
- [x] phone the signal operator
- [x] edge over the stop line and look for trains
- [x] park your vehicle and investigate.

Answer

 carry on waiting

If the lights at a level crossing continue to flash after a train has passed continue to wait, as there might be another train coming. Time seems to pass slowly when you're held up in a queue. Be patient and wait until the lights stop flashing.

Question

At toucan crossings, apart from pedestrians you should be aware of

Mark one answer

- [x] emergency vehicles emerging
- [x] buses pulling out
- [x] trams crossing in front
- [x] cyclists riding across.

Answer

 cyclists riding across

The use of cycles is being encouraged and more toucan crossings are being installed. These crossings enable pedestrians and cyclists to cross the path of other traffic. Watch out as cyclists will approach the crossing faster than a pedestrian.

Question
Who can use a toucan crossing?

Mark two answers

☒ Trains.

☒ Cyclists.

☒ Buses.

☒ Pedestrians.

☒ Trams.

Answers

☒ **Cyclists.**

☒ **Pedestrians.**

Toucan crossings are similar to pelican crossings. Cyclists share the crossing with pedestrians without the need to dismount. They're shown a green cycle when it's safe to cross.

Question
At a pelican crossing, what does a flashing amber light mean?

Mark one answer

☒ You must not move off until the lights stop flashing.

☒ You must give way to pedestrians still on the crossing.

☒ You can move off, even if pedestrians are still on the crossing.

☒ You must stop because the lights are about to change to red.

Answer

☒ **You must give way to pedestrians still on the crossing.**

If the road is clear then proceed. The green light will show after the flashing amber.

Question
You are on a busy main road and find that you are travelling in the wrong direction. What should you do?

Mark one answer

☒ Turn into a side road on the right and reverse into the main road.

☒ Make a U-turn in the main road.

☒ Make a 'three-point' turn in the main road.

☒ Turn round in a side road.

Answer

☒ **Turn round in a side road.**

Don't

• turn in a busy street

• reverse into a main road.

Find a quiet side road. Choose a place where you won't obstruct an entrance or exit, and look out for pedestrians and cyclists as well as other traffic.

Question

You may drive on a footpath

Mark one answer

☒ to overtake slow-moving traffic

☒ when the pavement is very wide

☒ if no pedestrians are near

☒ to get into a property.

Answer

☒ **to get into a property**

When you're crossing the pavement watch out for pedestrians and cyclists in both directions.

Question

You are parked in a busy high street. What is the safest way to turn your vehicle around to go the opposite way?

Mark one answer

☒ Find a quiet side road to turn round in.

☒ Drive into a side road and reverse into the main road.

☒ Get someone to stop the traffic.

☒ Do a U-turn.

Answer

☒ **Find a quiet side road to turn round in.**

You should carry out the manoeuvre without causing a hazard to other vehicles.

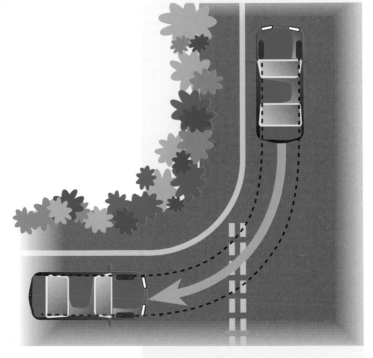

Question

You may remove your seat belt when carrying out a manoeuvre that involves

Mark one answer

- ☒ reversing
- ☒ a hill start
- ☒ an emergency stop
- ☒ driving slowly.

Answer

 ✗ **reversing**

Don't forget to click your seat belt back on when you've finished reversing.

Question

You must not reverse

Mark one answer

- ☒ for longer than necessary
- ☒ for more than a car's length
- ☒ into a side road
- ☒ in a built-up area.

Answer

 ✗ **for longer than necessary**

You may decide to turn your vehicle around by reversing into an opening or side road. When you reverse, always look behind and watch for pedestrians. Don't

- reverse for longer than is necessary
- reverse from a side road into a main road

Question

When you're NOT sure that it's safe to reverse your vehicle you should

Mark one answer

- ☒ use your horn.
- ☒ rev your engine.
- ☒ get out and check.
- ☒ reverse slowly.

Answer

✗ **get out and check.**

If you can't see all around your vehicle get out and have a look. You could also ask someone outside the vehicle to guide you. A small child could easily be hidden directly behind you. Don't take risks.

Question

When may you reverse from a side road into a main road?

Mark one answer

- ☒ Only if both roads are clear of traffic.
- ☒ Not at any time.
- ☒ At any time.
- ☒ Only if the main road is clear of traffic.

Answer

 ✗ **Not at any time.**

Don't reverse into a main road from a side road. The main road is likely to be busy and the traffic on it moving quickly. Cut down the risks by using a quiet side road to reverse into.

Question

You're reversing your vehicle into a side road. When would the greatest hazard to passing traffic occur?

Mark one answer

☒ After you've completed the manoeuvre.

☒ Just before you actually begin to manoeuvre.

☒ After you've entered the side road.

☒ When the front of your vehicle swings out.

Answer

☒ **When the front of your vehicle swings out.**

Always check road and traffic conditions in all directions. Act on what you see and wait if you need to.

This section looks at road and traffic signs.

The questions will ask you about

- road signs
- speed limits
- road markings
- regulations.

Question

You MUST obey signs giving orders. These signs are mostly in

Mark one answer

☒ green rectangles

☒ red triangles

☒ blue rectangles

☒ red circles.

Question

Traffic signs giving orders are generally which shape?

Mark one answer

☒   ☒

☒   ☒

Answer

☒ **red circles**

Traffic signs can be divided into three classes – those giving orders, those warning and those informing. On the road each class of sign has a different shape.

Answer

☒

Road signs in the shape of a circle give orders. Those with a red circle are mostly prohibitive. The stop sign is octagonal to give it greater prominence. These signs must always be obeyed.

Question

Which type of sign tells you NOT to do something?

Mark one answer

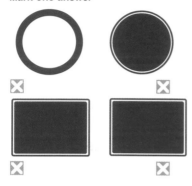

☒   ☒

☒   ☒

Question

What does this sign mean?

Mark one answer

☒ Maximum speed limit with traffic calming.

☒ Minimum speed limit with traffic calming.

☒ '20 cars only' parking zone.

☒ Only 20 cars allowed at any one time.

☒

Signs in the shape of a circle mean that you aren't allowed to do something. Study *Know Your Traffic Signs* to ensure that you understand the order you're shown.

Answer

☒ **Maximum speed limit with traffic calming.**

If you're driving in areas where there are likely to be pedestrians such as

- outside schools
- near parks
- residential areas
- shopping areas

be extra cautious and keep your speed down. Many local authorities have taken measures to slow traffic down by creating traffic calming measures such as speed humps. They're there for a reason: slow down.

Question

Which sign means no motor vehicles are allowed?

Mark one answer

Answer

Certain areas are set aside for pedestrians to walk free of traffic.

Question

What does this sign mean?

Mark one answer

- New speed limit 20 mph.
- No vehicles over 30 tonnes.
- Minimum speed limit 30 mph.
- End of 20 mph zone.

Answer

 End of 20 mph zone.

Where you see this sign the 20 mph restriction ends. Only increase your speed if it's safe to do so. Check all around and well down the road before increasing your speed.

Question
What does this sign mean?

Mark one answer

☒ No overtaking.

☒ No motor vehicles.

☒ Clearway (no stopping).

☒ Cars and motorcycles only.

Answer

✖ **No motor vehicles.**

Traffic may be prohibited from certain roads. A sign will indicate which types of vehicles aren't allowed to use it. Make sure that you know which signs apply to the vehicle you're using.

Question
What does this sign mean?

Mark one answer

☒ No parking.

☒ No road markings.

☒ No through road.

☒ No entry.

Answer

✖ **No entry.**

Not knowing the meaning of a road sign could lead you into a dangerous situation.

Question
What does this sign mean?

Mark one answer

☒ Bend to the right.

☒ Road on the right closed.

☒ No traffic from the right.

☒ No right turn.

Answer

✖ **No right turn.**

The road on the right might be a no entry or the sign could be there to allow the traffic on the main road to flow by stopping cars queuing to turn right.

Question

Which sign means 'no entry'?

Mark one answer

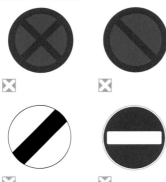

☒   ☒

☒   ☒

Question

What does this sign mean?

Mark one answer

☒   Route for trams only.

☒   Route for buses only.

☒   Parking for buses only.

☒   Parking for trams only.

Answer

Look out for traffic signs as you drive. Disobeying or not seeing a sign could not only be dangerous, but also an offence: you could be fined.

Answer

☒   **Route for trams only.**

Avoid blocking tram routes. Trams are fixed on their route and can't dodge around other vehicles and pedestrians. Modern trams travel quickly and are quiet so you might not hear them approaching.

Question

Which type of vehicle does this sign apply to?

Mark one answer

 Wide vehicles.

 Long vehicles.

High vehicles.

Heavy vehicles.

Answer

❌ **High vehicles.**

The triangular shapes at the top and bottom of the sign mean that the sign is showing you the restricted height.

Question

Which sign means NO motor vehicles allowed?

Mark one answer

Answer

This sign is used to enable pedestrians to walk free from traffic. It's often found in stopping areas.

Question

What does this sign mean?

Answer

❌ **Do not overtake.**

The 'no overtaking' sign is in the shape of a circle so you must obey this order. You may see it where there's a series of bends or the road is narrow.

Mark one answer

 Do not overtake.

Oncoming cars have priority.

Two-way traffic.

No right turn ahead.

Question
What does this sign mean?

Mark one answer

- [ ] You have priority.
- [ ] No motor vehicles.
- [ ] Two-way traffic.
- [ ] No overtaking.

Answer

✗ No overtaking.

Road signs that show no overtaking will be placed in locations where passing the vehicle in front is dangerous. If you see this sign don't attempt to overtake. The sign is there for a reason and you must obey it.

Question
What does this sign mean?

Mark one answer

- [ ] Keep in one lane.
- [ ] Priority to traffic coming towards you.
- [ ] Do not overtake.
- [ ] Form two lanes.

Answer

✗ Do not overtake.

If you're behind a slow-moving vehicle be patient. Wait until the restriction no longer applies and you can overtake safely.

Question

Which sign means no overtaking?

Mark one answer

Answer

This sign indicates that your view down the road is restricted, or there may be a junction ahead. For these reasons overtaking here would be dangerous. Don't take risks.

Question

What does this sign mean?

Mark one answer

- Waiting restrictions apply.
- Waiting permitted.
- National speed limit applies.
- Clearway (no stopping).

Answer

X Waiting restrictions apply.

There will be a plate or additional sign to tell you when the restrictions apply.

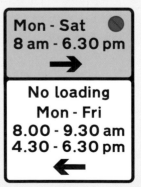

Question
What does this sign mean?

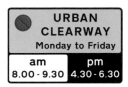

Mark one answer

☒ You can park on the days and times shown.

☒ No parking on the days and times shown.

☒ No parking at all from Monday to Friday.

☒ You can park at any time: the urban clearway ends.

Question
What does this sign mean?

Mark one answer

☒ End of restricted speed area.

☒ End of restricted parking area.

☒ End of clearway.

☒ End of cycle route.

Answer

❌ **No parking on the days and times shown.**

Before you leave your vehicle parked at the side of the road check that the space isn't restricted. Parking times vary from place to place so always check the sign before securing and leaving your car.

Answer

❌ **End of restricted parking area.**

Even though there are no restrictions make sure that you park where you won't cause an obstruction or endanger other road users.

Question
Which sign means 'no stopping'?

Mark one answer

Answer

Stopping where you see this sign is likely to cause congestion. Allow the traffic to flow by obeying the signs.

Question
What does this sign mean?

Mark one answer

- ☒ Roundabout.
- ☒ Crossroads.
- ☒ No stopping.
- ☒ No entry.

Answer

☒ No stopping.

This sign is in place to ensure a clear route for traffic. Don't stop except in an emergency.

Question
You see this sign ahead. It means

Mark one answer

- ☒ national speed limit applies
- ☒ waiting restrictions apply
- ☒ no stopping
- ☒ no entry.

Answer

☒ no stopping.

There are stretches of road where you aren't allowed to stop (unless in an emergency). These are called 'clearways'. You'll see this sign. Stopping where these restrictions apply may be dangerous and could cause an obstruction. Restrictions might apply for several miles and this may be indicated on the sign.

Question
What does this sign mean?

Mark one answer

☒ Distance to parking place ahead.

☒ Distance to public telephone ahead.

☒ Distance to public house ahead.

☒ Distance to passing place ahead.

Answer

☒ **Distance to parking place ahead.**

If you intend to stop and rest note this early indication. This sign allows you time to ask any passengers if they need to stop for any reason.

Question
What does this sign mean?

Mark one answer

☒ Vehicles may not park on the verge or footway.

☒ Vehicles may park on the left-hand side of the road only.

☒ Vehicles may park fully on the verge or footway.

☒ Vehicles may park on the right-hand side of the road only.

Answer

☒ **Vehicles may park fully on the verge or footway.**

In order to keep roads free from parked cars there are some areas where you're allowed to park on the verge. Only do this where you see the sign. Parking on verges or kerbs in other areas could lead to a fine.

Question

What does this traffic sign mean?

Mark one answer

- ☒ No overtaking allowed.
- ☒ Give priority to oncoming traffic.
- ☒ No U-turns allowed.
- ☒ One-way traffic only.

Question

What is the meaning of this traffic sign?

Mark one answer

- ☒ End of two-way road.
- ☒ Give priority to vehicles coming towards you.
- ☒ You have priority over vehicles coming towards you.
- ☒ Bus lane ahead.

Answer

☒ **Give priority to oncoming traffic.**

Priority signs are normally shown where the road is narrow and there isn't enough room for two vehicles to pass, such as

- a narrow bridge
- at roadworks
- a width restriction.

Make sure that you know who has priority. Comply with the sign and don't force a right of way. Show courtesy and consideration to other road users.

Answer

☒ **You have priority over vehicles coming towards you.**

Don't force a right of way. Show courtesy and consideration to other road users.

Question

Which sign means 'traffic has priority over oncoming vehicles'?

Mark one answer

Answer

Even though you may have priority, give way if proceeding is likely to cause an accident, congestion or confrontation.

Question

What does this sign mean?

Mark one answer

- ☒ No overtaking.
- ☒ You are entering a one-way street.
- ☒ Two-way traffic ahead.
- ☒ You have priority over vehicles from the opposite direction.

Answer

☒ **You have priority over vehicles from the opposite direction.**

Don't force the issue. Slow down and give way to avoid confrontation or an accident.

Question
What should you do when you see this sign?

Mark one answer

☒ Stop, ONLY if traffic is approaching.

☒ Stop, even if the road is clear.

☒ Stop, ONLY if children are waiting to cross.

☒ Stop, ONLY if a red light is showing.

Question
What shape is a stop sign at a junction?

Mark one answer

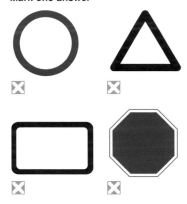

☒   ☒

☒   ☒

Answer
☒ **Stop, even if the road is clear.**

A stop sign is shown on an octagonal-shaped background. The sign will be at a junction where visibility is restricted or there's heavy traffic.

IT MUST BE OBEYED. YOU MUST STOP.

Practise good all-round observation before moving off.

Answer

The stop sign is distinctive and the only sign of this shape. You must stop and make effective observation before proceeding.

Question

Which shape of traffic sign means that you must stop?

Mark one answer

Answer

You won't have enough time to make effective observation without stopping. Stop, and don't emerge until you're sure that it's safe.

Question

What does this sign mean?

Mark one answer

- ☒ Service area 30 miles ahead.
- ☒ Maximum speed 30 mph.
- ☒ Minimum speed 30 mph.
- ☒ Lay-by 30 miles ahead.

Answer

 Minimum speed 30 mph.

This sign is shown where slow-moving vehicles would impede the flow of traffic. However, if you need to slow down to avoid a potential accident you should do so.

Question
At a mini-roundabout you should

Mark one answer

☒ give way to traffic from the right

☒ give way to traffic from the left

☒ give way to traffic from the other way

☒ stop even when empty.

Question
What does this sign mean?

Mark one answer

☒ Give way to oncoming vehicles.

☒ Approaching traffic passes you on both sides.

☒ Turn off at the next available junction.

☒ Pass either side to get to the same destination.

Question
What does this sign mean?

Mark one answer

☒ Route for trams.

☒ Give way to trams.

☒ Route for buses.

☒ Give way to buses.

Answer
☒ give way to traffic from the right

Look out for other traffic as you approach. Vehicles entering the mini-roundabout from your left or ahead might prevent traffic on your right from proceeding. Watch for their signals and continue if it's safe to do so.

Answer
☒ Pass either side to get to the same destination.

These signs are often seen in one-way streets that have more than one lane. Use the route that's the most convenient and doesn't require a late change of direction.

Answer
☒ Route for trams.

Take extra care when you first encounter trams. Look out for road markings and signs that alert you to them. Modern trams are very quiet and you may not hear them approaching.

Question
What does a circular traffic sign with a blue background do?

Mark one answer

☒ Give warning of a motorway ahead.

☒ Give directions to a car park.

☒ Give motorway information.

☒ Give an instruction.

Answer
☒ **Give an instruction.**

Signs with blue circles give a positive instruction. They will often be seen in towns or urban areas. For example

mini-roundabout

pass either side.

Question
Which of these signs means that you are entering a one-way street?

Mark one answer

☒

☒

☒

☒

Answer
☒

If the road has two lanes you can use either lane and overtake on either side. Use the lane that's more convenient for your destination.

Question

Where would you see a contraflow bus and cycle lane?

Mark one answer

⊠ On a dual carriageway.

⊠ On a roundabout.

⊠ On an urban motorway.

⊠ On a one-way street.

Question

What does this sign mean?

Mark one answer

⊠ Bus station on the right.

⊠ Contraflow bus lane.

⊠ With-flow bus lane.

⊠ Give way to buses.

Question

What does this sign mean?

Mark one answer

⊠ With-flow bus and cycle lane.

⊠ Contraflow bus and cycle lane.

⊠ No buses and cycles allowed.

⊠ No waiting for buses and cycles.

Answer

❌ **On a one-way street.**

'Contraflow' means that the bus or cycle lane is going in the opposite direction to the other lanes in the road. Don't drive in or straddle these lanes.

Answer

❌ **Contraflow bus lane.**

There will also be markings on the road surface to indicate the bus lane. Don't use this lane for parking or overtaking.

Answer

❌ **With-flow bus and cycle lane.**

In this case buses and cycles may travel in this lane in the same direction as other traffic. There may be times shown on the sign to indicate when the lane is in use.

Question

What does a sign with a brown background show?

Mark one answer

☒ Tourist directions.

☒ Primary roads.

☒ Motorway routes.

☒ Minor routes.

Answer

☒ **Tourist directions.**

Signs with a brown background give directions to places of interest. They will often be seen on the motorway directing you along the easiest route.

Question

What are triangular signs for?

Mark one answer

☒ To give warnings.

☒ To give information.

☒ To give orders.

☒ To give directions.

Answer

☒ **To give warnings.**

This type of sign will tell you about the road ahead and what to expect. Get into the habit of checking each sign that you pass. They will warn you of the hazards ahead.

Question

What does this sign mean?

Mark one answer

☒ Turn left ahead.

☒ T-junction.

☒ No through road.

☒ Give way.

Answer

☒ **T-junction.**

Look well down the road and check the road signs as you drive. You'll then be able to anticipate any junction hazards.

Question
What does this sign mean?

Mark one answer
- ☒ Crossroads.
- ☒ Level crossing with gate.
- ☒ Level crossing without gate.
- ☒ Ahead only.

Answer
✗ Crossroads.

The priority through the junction is shown by the broader line. However, be aware of the danger when other traffic is crossing a major road.

Question
What does this sign mean?

Mark one answer
- ☒ Ring road.
- ☒ Mini-roundabout.
- ☒ Restriction ends.
- ☒ Roundabout.

Answer
✗ Roundabout.

Prepare yourself for approaching hazards by checking signs as you drive.

Decide which exit you wish to take. Prepare to position your vehicle correctly as you approach the roundabout.

Question
Which FOUR of these would be indicated by a triangular road sign?

Mark four answers
- ☒ Road narrows.
- ☒ Ahead only.
- ☒ Low bridge.
- ☒ Minimum speed.
- ☒ Children crossing.
- ☒ T-junction.

Answers
✗ Road narrows.
✗ Low bridge.
✗ Children crossing.
✗ T-junction.

Question
What does this sign mean?

Mark one answer

☒ Cyclists must dismount.

☒ Bicycles are not allowed.

☒ You are approaching a cycle route.

☒ Walking is not allowed.

Answer

☒ **You are approaching a cycle route.**

Where there's a cycle route a sign will show a bicycle in a red warning triangle. Watch out for children on bicycles and cyclists rejoining the main road.

Question
What does this sign mean?

Mark one answer

☒ No footpath ahead.

☒ Pedestrians only ahead.

☒ Pedestrian crossing ahead.

☒ School crossing ahead.

Answer

☒ **Pedestrian crossing ahead.**

There are many signs relating to pedestrians. Study *The Highway Code* and *Know Your Traffic Signs*. Some of the signs look similar but give different warnings. Make a mental note as you drive so that you're prepared for any potential hazard.

Question
What does this sign mean?

Mark one answer

☒ School crossing patrol.

☒ No pedestrians allowed.

☒ Pedestrian zone – no vehicles.

☒ Pedestrian crossing ahead.

Answer

☒ **Pedestrian crossing ahead.**

Look well ahead and be ready to stop for any pedestrians crossing the road. Also check the pavements for anyone who looks like they might step off into the road.

Question

Which of these signs means there is a double bend ahead?

Mark one answer

Answer

Triangular signs give you a warning of hazards ahead. They're there to give you time to adjust your speed and drive accordingly.

Question

What does this sign mean?

Mark one answer

 Wait at the barriers.

 Wait at the crossroads.

 Give way to trams.

 Give way to farm vehicles.

Answer

 Give way to trams.

Obey the 'give way' signs. Trams are unable to steer around you or change their specific route.

Question

What does this sign mean?

Mark one answer

☒ Humpback bridge.

☒ Humps in the road.

☒ Entrance to tunnel.

☒ Steep hill upwards.

Answer

 Humps in the road.

These have been put in place to slow the traffic down. They're usually found in residential areas. Slow down and drive at an appropriate speed.

Question

What does this sign mean?

Mark one answer

☒ Low bridge ahead.

☒ Tunnel ahead.

☒ Ancient monument ahead.

☒ Accident black spot ahead.

Answer

 Tunnel ahead.

Be prepared to switch on your headlights, if required. Reduce your speed. Your eyes might need to adjust to the sudden darkness.

Question

What does this sign mean?

Mark one answer

☒ Two-way traffic ahead.

☒ Two-way traffic crossing a one-way street.

☒ Two-way traffic over a bridge.

☒ Two-way traffic crosses a two-way road.

Answer

Two-way traffic crossing a one-way street.

Be prepared for traffic approaching from junctions on either side of you.

Try to avoid unnecessary changing of lanes just before the junction.

Question

Which sign means 'two-way traffic crosses a one-way road'?

Mark one answer

Answer

Traffic could be joining the road you're in from either direction. Unless you need to turn, don't change lanes as you approach the junction.

Question

Which of these signs means the end of a dual carriageway?

Mark one answer

Answer

If you're travelling in the right-hand lane, prepare and move over into the left-lane as soon as it's safe to do so.

Question
What does this sign mean?

Mark one answer

☒ End of dual carriageway.

☒ Tall bridge.

☒ Road narrows.

☒ End of narrow bridge.

Answer

✖ **End of dual carriageway.**

Don't leave moving into the left-hand lane until the last moment. Early planning will prevent you having to rely on other traffic letting you in.

Question
What does this sign mean?

Mark one answer

☒ Two-way traffic ahead across a one-way street.

☒ Traffic approaching you has priority.

☒ Two-way traffic straight ahead.

☒ Motorway contraflow system ahead.

Answer

✖ **Two-way traffic straight ahead.**

This sign may be at the end of a dual carriageway or a one-way street. The sign is there to warn you of oncoming traffic.

Question
What does this sign mean?

Mark one answer

☒ Crosswinds.

☒ Road noise.

☒ Airport.

☒ Adverse camber.

Answer

✖ **Crosswinds.**

Where weather conditions are often bad, signs will give you a warning. A sign with a picture of a wind-sock will indicate there may be strong crosswinds. This sign is often found on exposed roads.

Question

What does this traffic sign mean?

Mark one answer

☒ Slippery road ahead.

☒ Tyres liable to punctures ahead.

☒ Danger ahead.

☒ Service area ahead.

Question

You are about to overtake when you see this sign. You should

Hidden dip

Mark one answer

☒ overtake the other driver as quickly as possible

☒ move to the right to get a better view

☒ switch your headlights on before overtaking

☒ hold back until you can see clearly ahead.

Answer

☒ **Danger ahead.**

A sign showing an exclamation mark (!) will alert you to the likelihood of danger ahead. Be ready for any situation that requires you to reduce your speed.

Answer

☒ **hold back until you can see clearly ahead**

You won't be able to see any hazards that might be out of sight in the dip.

Imagine there might be

• cyclists

• horse riders

• parked vehicles

• pedestrians.

There might be oncoming traffic to deal with, too.

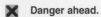

Question
What does this sign mean?

Mark one answer

- [ ] Quayside or river bank.
- [ ] Steep hill downwards.
- [ ] Slippery road.
- [ ] Road liable to flooding.

Answer

 Quayside or river bank.

Be aware that the road surface in this location is likely to be wet and slippery.

Question
What does this sign mean?

Mark one answer

- [ ] Uneven road surface.
- [ ] Bridge over the road.
- [ ] Road ahead ends.
- [ ] Water across the road.

Answer

 Water across the road.

This sign is found where a shallow stream crosses the road. Heavy rainfall could increase the flow of water. If the water looks too deep or the stream has swelled over a large distance, stop and find another route.

Question
What does this sign mean?

Mark one answer

- [ ] Humpback bridge.
- [ ] Traffic calming hump.
- [ ] Low bridge.
- [ ] Uneven road.

Answer

 Humpback bridge.

Slow right down. Driving over a humpback bridge too fast could cause your wheels to leave the road surface and result in a loss of control.

Question
What does this sign mean?

Mark one answer

 Turn left for parking area.

No through road on the left.

No entry for traffic turning left.

Turn left for ferry terminal.

Question
Which sign means 'no through road'?

Mark one answer

Question
Which is the sign for a ring road?

Mark one answer

Answer

❌ **No through road on the left.**

Signs are there to help you to drive safely and to help you to avoid making late decisions. If you intend to take a left turn this sign shows you that you can't get through to another route.

Answer
❌

This sign is found at the entrance to the junction.

Answer
❌

Ring roads are designed to relieve congestion in towns and cities.

Question
What does this sign mean?

Mark one answer

- [ ] Route for lorries.
- [ ] Ring road.
- [ ] Rest area.
- [ ] Roundabout.

Answer

✖ Ring road.

Signs are also designed to give you advice. Ring road signs direct traffic around major towns and cities. Ring roads help the traffic to flow and ease congestion in town centres.

Question
What does this sign mean?

Mark one answer

- [ ] Railway station.
- [ ] Route for cyclists.
- [ ] Ring road.
- [ ] Scenic route.

Answer

✖ Ring road.

These routes help through traffic to avoid town centres. This relieves congestion in the town and helps through traffic to flow.

Question
What does this sign mean?

Mark one answer

- [ ] Hilly road.
- [ ] Humps in road.
- [ ] Holiday route.
- [ ] Hospital route.

Answer

✖ Holiday route.

In some areas where the volume of traffic increases during the summer months signs show a route that diverts traffic away from town centres. This helps the traffic to flow, decreasing queues.

Question
What does this sign mean?

Mark one answer

☒ The right-hand lane ahead is narrow.

☒ Right-hand lane for buses only.

☒ No turning to the right.

☒ The right-hand lane is closed.

Answer

☒ **The right-hand lane is closed.**

Temporary signs may tell you about roadworks or lane restrictions. Look well ahead. If you have to change lanes do so in good time.

Question
What does this sign mean?

Mark one answer

☒ Change to the left lane.

☒ Leave at the next exit.

☒ Contraflow system.

☒ One-way street.

Answer

☒ **Contraflow system.**

If you use the right-hand lane, you'll be travelling with no permanent barrier between your vehicle and the traffic coming towards you. Observe speed limits and keep a good distance from the car ahead.

Question

You see this traffic light ahead. Which light(s) will come on next?

Answer

 Red alone.

At junctions controlled by traffic lights you must stop behind the white line until the lights change to green. Don't

- move forward when the red and amber lights are showing together
- proceed when the light is green if your exit road is blocked.

If you're approaching traffic lights that are visible from a distance and the light has been green for some time it's likely to change. Try to anticipate this. Be ready to slow down and stop.

Mark one answer

- ☒ Red alone.
- ☒ Red and amber together.
- ☒ Green and amber together.
- ☒ Green alone.

Question

You are approaching a red traffic light. The signal will change from red to

Answer

☒ **red and amber, then green**

If you know which light is going to show next you can plan your approach accordingly. This will prevent excessive braking or hesitation at the junction.

Mark one answer

- ☒ red and amber, then green
- ☒ green, then amber
- ☒ amber, then green
- ☒ green and amber, then green.

Question

A red traffic light means

Mark one answer

- [x] you should stop unless turning left
- [x] stop, if you are able to brake safely
- [x] you must stop and wait behind the stop line
- [x] proceed with caution.

Question

At traffic lights, amber on its own means

Mark one answer

- [x] prepare to go
- [x] go if the way is clear
- [x] go if no pedestrians are crossing
- [x] stop at the stop line.

Answer

[x] you must stop and wait behind the stop line

Learn the sequence of traffic lights.

RED means stop and wait behind the stop line.

RED-and-AMBER also means stop. Don't go until the green light shows.

GREEN means you may go if your way is clear. Don't proceed if your exit road is blocked, and don't block the junction. Look out for pedestrians.

AMBER means stop at the stop line. You may go if the amber light appears after you've crossed the stop line or you're so close to it that to pull up might cause an accident.

Answer

[x] stop at the stop line

If the lights have been on green for a while they're likely to change to red as you approach. Anticipate this so that you're able to stop in time.

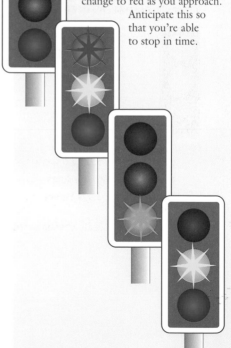

Question
A red traffic light means

Answer

 you must stop behind the white stop line

The white line is positioned so that pedestrians have room to cross in front of waiting vehicles. If pedestrians are crossing make sure your handbrake is on.

Mark one answer

☒ you must stop behind the white stop line

☒ you may drive straight on if there is no other traffic

☒ you may turn left if it is safe to do so

☒ you must slow down and prepare to stop if traffic has started to cross.

Question
You are approaching traffic lights. Red and amber are showing. This means

Answer

☒ **wait for the green light before you pass the lights**

Other traffic might still be clearing the junction. Don't take risks.

Mark one answer

☒ pass the lights if the road is clear

☒ there is a fault with the lights – take care

☒ wait for the green light before you pass the lights

☒ the lights are about to change to red.

Question

You are at a junction controlled by traffic lights. When should you NOT proceed at green?

Mark one answer

☒ When pedestrians are waiting to cross.

☒ When your exit from the junction is blocked.

☒ When you think the lights may be about to change.

☒ When you intend to turn right.

Question

You are in the left-hand lane at traffic lights. You are waiting to turn left. At which of these traffic lights must you NOT move on?

Mark one answer

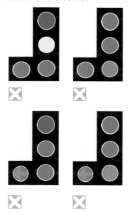

☒　　　☒

☒　　　☒

Answer

☒ **When your exit from the junction is blocked.**

As you approach the lights look into the road you wish to take. Only proceed if your exit road is clear. If the road is blocked hold back, even if you have to wait for the next green signal.

Answer

At some junctions there may be a separate signal for each lane. These are called 'filter' lights. They're designed to help traffic flow at major junctions. Make sure that you're in the correct lane and proceed if the green light shows.

Question
What does this sign mean?

Answer

❌ **Traffic lights out of order.**

Where traffic lights are out of order you might see this sign. Proceed with caution as nobody has priority at the junction.

Mark one answer

☒ Traffic lights out of order.

☒ Amber signal out of order.

☒ Temporary traffic lights ahead.

☒ New traffic lights ahead.

Question
When traffic lights are out of order, who has priority?

Mark one answer

☒ Traffic going straight on.

☒ Traffic turning right.

☒ Nobody.

☒ Traffic turning left.

Answer

❌ **Nobody.**

Treat the junction as an unmarked cross-roads. Deal with the situation with caution.

Question
These flashing red lights mean STOP. In which THREE of the following places could you find them?

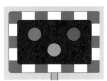

Answers

❌ **Lifting bridges.**

❌ **Level crossings.**

❌ **Fire stations.**

Don't take risks by trying to beat the lights, even if it's clear. You must stop.

Mark three answers

☒ Pelican crossings.

☒ Lifting bridges.

☒ Zebra crossings.

☒ Level crossings.

☒ Motorway exits.

☒ Fire stations.

Question
What do these zigzag lines at pedestrian crossings mean?

Mark one answer

- [ ] No parking at any time.
- [ ] Parking allowed only for a short time.
- [ ] Slow down to 20 mph.
- [ ] Sounding horns is not allowed.

Answer
✗ No parking at any time.

The approach to hazards may be marked with signs on the road surface. The approach to a pedestrian crossing is marked with zigzag lines.

Don't

- park on them
- overtake the leading vehicle when approaching the crossing.

Parking here will block the view for pedestrians and the approaching traffic.

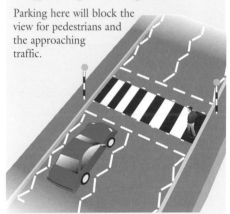

Question
You are approaching a zebra crossing where pedestrians are waiting. Which arm signal might you give?

Mark one answer

Answer
✗

A 'slowing down' signal will indicate your intentions to oncoming and following vehicles. Be aware that pedestrians might start to cross as soon as they see this signal.

Question

When may you cross a double solid white line in the middle of the road?

Mark one answer

☒ To pass traffic that is queuing back at a junction.

☒ To pass a car signalling to turn left ahead.

☒ To pass a road maintenance vehicle travelling at 10 mph or less.

☒ To pass a vehicle that is towing a trailer.

Answer

☒ **To pass a road maintenance vehicle travelling at 10 mph or less.**

Only overtake such a vehicle if you're sure that you can complete the manoeuvre safely. Keep well back before you overtake so that you have a clear view of the road. Double solid white lines indicate that there are hazards, such as bends in the road or junctions, so be extra cautious.

Question

A white line like this along the centre of the road is a

Mark one answer

☒ bus lane marking

☒ hazard warning

☒ 'give way' marking

☒ lane marking.

Answer

☒ **hazard warning**

Make a note of hazard lines as you drive. Look well ahead and around so that you're prepared for any potential dangers.

Question

What does this road marking mean?

Mark one answer

☒ Do not cross the line.

☒ No stopping allowed.

☒ You are approaching a hazard.

☒ No overtaking allowed.

Answer

☒ **You are approaching a hazard.**

Road markings will warn you of a hazard ahead. A single broken line, with long markings and short gaps, along the centre of the road is a hazard warning line. Don't cross it unless you can see that the road is clear WELL ahead.

Question

Where would you see this road marking?

Mark one answer

- ☒ At traffic lights.
- ☒ On road humps.
- ☒ Near a level crossing.
- ☒ At a box junction.

Answer

☒ **On road humps.**

Due to the dark colour of the road, changes in surface aren't easily seen. White triangles painted on the road surface give you an indication of where there are road humps.

Question

Which is a hazard warning line?

Mark one answer

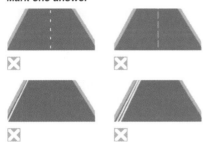

Answer

☒

Look out for places where the single broken line on the road surface gets longer. This will mean there's a hazard ahead.

Question

What does this sign mean?

Mark one answer

- ☒ Leave motorway at next exit.
- ☒ Lane for heavy and slow vehicles.
- ☒ All lorries use the hard shoulder.
- ☒ Rest area for lorries.

Answer

☒ **Lane for heavy and slow vehicles.**

Where there's a long, steep, uphill gradient on a motorway there may be a crawler lane. This type of lane helps the traffic to flow by diverting the slower heavy vehicles into an extra lane on the left.

Question

At this junction there is a stop sign with a solid white line on the road surface. Why is there a stop sign here?

Mark one answer

☒ Speed on the major road is de-restricted.

☒ It is a busy junction.

☒ Visibility along the major road is restricted.

☒ There are hazard warning lines in the centre of the road.

Question

You see this line across the road at the entrance to a roundabout. What does it mean?

Mark one answer

☒ Give way to traffic from the right.

☒ Traffic from the left has right of way.

☒ You have right of way.

☒ Stop at the line.

Answer

☒ **Visibility along the major road is restricted.**

If your view is restricted at a road junction you must stop. There may also be a stop sign. Don't emerge until you're sure there's no traffic approaching.

IF YOU DON'T KNOW, DON'T GO.

Answer

☒ **Give way to traffic from the right.**

Slow down as you approach, checking the traffic as you do so. If you need to stop and give way, stay behind the broken line until it is safe to emerge onto the roundabout.

Question

Where would you find this road marking?

Mark one answer

☒ At a railway crossing.

☒ At a junction.

☒ On a motorway.

☒ On a pedestrian crossing.

Question

How will a police officer in a patrol vehicle get you to stop?

Mark one answer

☒ Flash the headlights, indicate left and point to the left.

☒ Wait until you stop, then approach you.

☒ Use the siren, overtake, cut in front and stop.

☒ Pull alongside you, use the siren and wave you to stop.

Question

There is a police car following you. The police officer flashes the headlights and points to the left. What should you do?

Mark one answer

☒ Turn at the next left.

☒ Pull up on the left.

☒ Stop immediately.

☒ Move over to the left.

Answer

❌ **At a junction.**

This marking indicates the direction in which the traffic should flow.

Answer

❌ **Flash the headlights, indicate left and point to the left.**

You must obey signals given by the police. If a police officer in a patrol vehicle wants you to stop he or she will indicate this without causing danger to you or other traffic.

Answer

❌ **Pull up on the left.**

You must pull up on the left, as soon as it's safe to do so, and switch off your engine.

Question

You approach a junction. The traffic lights are not working. A police officer gives this signal. You should

Mark one answer

- [ ] turn left only
- [ ] turn right only
- [ ] stop level with the officer's arm
- [ ] stop at the stop line.

Answer

❌ **stop at the stop line**

If a police officer or traffic wardens are directing traffic you must obey them. They will use the arm signals shown in *The Highway Code*. Learn what these mean and act accordingly.

Question

The driver of the car in front is giving this arm signal. What does it mean?

Mark one answer

- [ ] The driver is slowing down.
- [ ] The driver intends to turn right.
- [ ] The driver wishes to overtake.
- [ ] The driver intends to turn left.

Answer

❌ **The driver intends to turn left.**

There might be an occasion where another driver uses a hand signal. This may be because the vehicle's indicators are obscured by other traffic. In order for such signals to be effective all drivers should know the meaning of them.

Be aware that the 'left turn' signal might look similar to the 'slowing down' signal.

Question

The driver of this car is giving a hand signal. What is he about to do?

Answer

  Turn to the left.

This could be used where there is a complicated junction and you wish to make your intentions clear.

For hand signals to be effective all road users should know their meaning.

Mark one answer

- ☒ Turn to the left.
- ☒ Turn to the right.
- ☒ Go straight ahead.
- ☒ Let pedestrians cross.

Question

Which arm signal tells a following vehicle that you intend to turn left?

Mark one answer

- ☒
- ☒
- ☒
- ☒

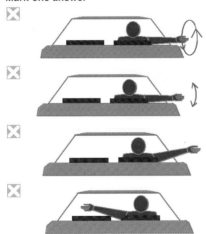

Answer

There may be occasions when you need to give an arm signal. For example

- where other road users can't see your indicators
- in bright sunshine, when your indicator may be difficult to see
- to reinforce a signal at a complex road layout.

Make sure that they're clear, correct and decisive.

Question
How should you give an arm signal to turn left?

Mark one answer

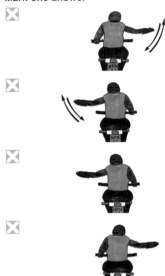

Answer

Arm signals are very effective during daylight, especially when you're wearing bright clothing.

Practise giving arm signals when you're learning. You need to be able to keep full control of your machine with one hand off the handlebars.

Question
You are giving an arm signal ready to turn left. Why should you NOT continue with the arm signal while you turn?

Answer

 Because you will have less steering control.

Don't maintain an arm signal when turning. You should have full control of your machine at all times.

Mark one answer

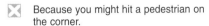

Because you might hit a pedestrian on the corner.

Because you will have less steering control.

Because you will need to keep the clutch applied.

Because other motorists will think that you are stopping on the corner.

Question
Your indicators are difficult to see due to bright sunshine. When using them you should

Mark one answer

☒ also give an arm signal

☒ sound your horn

☒ flash your headlamp

☒ keep both hands on the handlebars.

Answer

☒ **also give an arm signal**

Arm signals are effective when you aren't sure that your indicators can be seen by other road users. Make sure that your signal is decisive, and return your hand to the handlebars before you turn.

Question
You want to turn right at a junction but you think that your indicators cannot be seen clearly. What should you do?

Mark one answer

☒ Get out and check if your indicators can be seen.

☒ Stay in the left-hand lane.

☒ Keep well over to the right.

☒ Give an arm signal as well as an indicator signal.

Answer

☒ **Give an arm signal as well as an indicator signal.**

If you think that your indicators can't be seen clearly due to other vehicles obscuring them, make sure that your signal is seen by using an arm signal too.

Question
When may you sound the horn on your vehicle?

Mark one answer

☒ To give you right of way.

☒ To attract a friend's attention.

☒ To warn other drivers of your presence.

☒ To make slower drivers move over.

Answer

☒ **To warn other drivers of your presence.**

Don't use the horn aggressively. You must not sound it

• between 11.30 pm and 7 am

• when your vehicle's stationary

unless a moving vehicle poses a danger.

Question
When motorists flash their headlights at you it means

Mark one answer

☒ that there is a radar speed trap ahead

☒ that they are giving way to you

☒ that they are warning you of their presence

☒ that there is something wrong with your vehicle.

Answer

☒ **that they are warning you of their presence**

If other drivers flash their headlights this isn't a signal to show priority. The flashing of headlights has the same meaning as sounding the horn – it's a warning of their presence.

Question

Why should you make sure that you have cancelled your indicators after turning?

Mark one answer

☒ To avoid flattening the battery.

☒ To avoid misleading other road users.

☒ To avoid dazzling other road users.

☒ To avoid damage to the indicator relay.

Answer

❌ **To avoid misleading other road users.**

If you haven't taken a sharp turn your indicators might not turn off automatically. Be aware of this if you've used them for slight deviations, such as passing parked vehicles.

Question

You are waiting at a T-junction. A vehicle is coming from the right with the left signal flashing. What should you do?

Mark one answer

☒ Move out and accelerate hard.

☒ Wait until the vehicle starts to turn in.

☒ Pull out before the vehicle reaches the junction.

☒ Move out slowly.

Answer

❌ **Wait until the vehicle starts to turn in.**

Try to anticipate the actions of other road users. Their signals might be misleading.

When you're waiting at a junction don't emerge if you'll impede the progress of other traffic. Pulling out safely calls for accurate judgement.

Question

Where would you see these road markings?

Mark one answer

☒ At a level crossing.

☒ On a motorway slip road.

☒ At a pedestrian crossing.

☒ On a single-track road.

Answer

❌ **On a motorway slip road.**

You must not enter into the area marked except in an emergency.

Question

When may you use hazard warning lights when driving?

Mark one answer

- Instead of sounding the horn in a built-up area between 11.30 pm and 7 am.
- On a motorway or unrestricted dual carriageway, to warn of a hazard ahead.
- On rural routes, after a warning sign of animals.
- On the approach to toucan crossings, where cyclists are waiting to cross.

Answer

 On a motorway or unrestricted dual carriageway to warn of a hazard ahead.

Where there's queuing traffic ahead and you have to slow down and maybe stop, showing your hazard warning lights will alert the traffic behind to the situation. Don't forget to switch them off as the queue forms behind you.

Question

When may you NOT overtake on the left?

Mark one answer

- On a free-flowing motorway or dual carriageway.
- When the traffic is moving slowly in queues.
- On a one-way street.
- When the car in front is signalling to turn right.

Answer

 On a free-flowing motorway or dual carriageway.

You may only overtake on the left

- when traffic is moving slowly in queues
- when a vehicle ahead is positioned to turn right and there's room to pass on the left
- in a one-way street.

Don't overtake on the left if the traffic on a dual carriageway is flowing freely. Other road users won't anticipate your action.

Question

You are driving on a motorway. There is a slow-moving vehicle ahead. On the back you see this sign. You should

Mark one answer

- pass on the right
- pass on the left
- leave at the next exit
- drive no further.

Answer

 pass on the left

You'll have to change lanes in order to pass the vehicle. Use your mirror and signal. If it's safe to do so move over into the lane on your left. Look well down the road so that you can spot such hazards early, leaving you time to complete the manoeuvre safely.

Question
What does this motorway sign mean?

Mark one answer

- ☒ Change to the lane on your left.
- ☒ Leave the motorway at the next exit.
- ☒ Change to the opposite carriageway.
- ☒ Pull up on the hard shoulder.

Answer

☒ **Change to the lane on your left.**

On the motorway, signs might show temporary warnings. This allows for different traffic or weather conditions and might indicate

- lane closures
- speed limits
- weather warnings.

Question
What does this motorway sign mean?

Mark one answer

- ☒ Temporary minimum speed 50 mph.
- ☒ No services for 50 miles.
- ☒ Obstruction 50 metres (165 feet) ahead.
- ☒ Temporary maximum speed 50 mph.

Answer

☒ **Temporary maximum speed 50 mph.**

Look out for signs above your lane or on the central reserve. These will give you important information or warnings about the road ahead.

Due to the high speeds of motorway traffic these signs may light up some distance from any hazard. Don't ignore the signs just because the road looks clear to you.

Question
What does this sign mean?

Mark one answer

- ☒ Through traffic to use left lane.
- ☒ Right-hand lane T-junction only.
- ☒ Right-hand lane closed ahead.
- ☒ 11 tonne weight limit.

Answer

☒ **Right-hand lane closed ahead.**

Move over as soon as you see the sign and it's safe to do so. Don't stay in the lane, which is closed ahead, until the last moment to beat a queue of traffic.

Question
On a motorway this sign means

Mark one answer

☒ move over onto the hard shoulder

☒ pass a temporary obstruction on the left

☒ leave the motorway at the next exit

☒ move to the lane on your left.

Answer

☒ **move to the lane on your left**

If signs instruct you to change lanes do so in good time.

Question
What does '25' mean on this motorway sign?

Mark one answer

☒ The distance to the nearest town.

☒ The route number of the road.

☒ The number of the next junction.

☒ The speed limit on the slip road.

Answer

☒ **The number of the next junction.**

Before you set out on your journey use a road map to plan your route. You should give yourself enough time to get into the correct lane for the exit that you wish to take. Uncertainty at road junctions can lead to danger.

Question
You are driving on a motorway. Red flashing lights appear above your lane. What should you do?

Mark one answer

☒ Continue in that lane and await further information.

☒ Go no further in that lane.

☒ Drive onto the hard shoulder.

☒ Stop and wait for an instruction to proceed.

Answer

☒ **Go no further in that lane.**

If flashing red lights appear above, and all lanes are shown as blocked, STOP even if others don't.

Question
The right-hand lane of a three-lane motorway is

Mark one answer

☒ for lorries only

☒ an overtaking lane

☒ the right-turn lane

☒ an acceleration lane.

Answer

☒ **an overtaking lane**

Motorways today can become very busy. If a vehicle in the right-hand lane is preventing traffic to the rear from overtaking, or is travelling at a slower speed than those on the nearside, bunching can occur. This means that drivers will begin to travel too close to the vehicle in front of them. If you aren't overtaking, use the left-hand lane.

Question
Where can you find reflective amber studs on a motorway?

Mark one answer

☒ Separating the slip road from the motorway.

☒ On the left-hand edge of the road.

☒ On the right-hand edge of the road.

☒ Separating the lanes.

Answer

☒ **On the right-hand edge of the road.**

At night or in poor visibility reflective studs on the road will help you to judge your position on the carriageway.

Question
Where on a motorway would you find green reflective studs?

Mark one answer

☒ Separating driving lanes.

☒ Between the hard shoulder and the carriageway.

☒ At slip road entrances and exits.

☒ Between the carriageway and the central reservation.

Answer

☒ **At slip road entrances and exits.**

Knowing the colours of the reflective studs on the road will help you in foggy conditions or when visibility is poor.

Question

You are travelling along a motorway. You see this sign. You should

Mark one answer

- ☒ leave the motorway at the next exit
- ☒ turn left immediately
- ☒ change lane
- ☒ move onto the hard shoulder.

Answer

☒ **leave the motorway at the next exit**

You'll see this sign if the motorway is closed ahead. When you see it prepare to get into the nearside lane so that you can take the exit safely. Don't leave it to the last moment.

Question

What does this sign mean?

Mark one answer

- ☒ No motor vehicles.
- ☒ End of motorway.
- ☒ No through road.
- ☒ End of bus lane.

Answer

☒ **End of motorway.**

When you leave the motorway make sure that you check your speedometer. You may be going faster than you realise. Slow down using the slip road. Look out for speed limit signs.

Question

Which of these signs means that the national speed limit applies?

Mark one answer

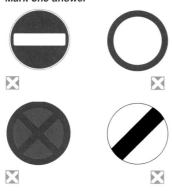

Answer

You should know the speed limit for the road that you're travelling on and the vehicle that you're driving. Study your copy of *The Highway Code*, where the limits are clearly shown.

Question

What is the maximum speed on a single carriageway road?

Mark one answer

- ☒ 50 mph.
- ☒ 60 mph.
- ☒ 40 mph.
- ☒ 70 mph.

Answer

 60 mph.

If you're travelling on a dual carriageway that's reduced to a single lane cut your speed gradually so that you aren't exceeding the limit as you enter. There might not be a sign to remind you of the limit, so learn the speed limits.

This section looks at the documents needed for drivers and their vehicles.

The questions will ask you about

- licences

- insurance

- MOT test certificates.

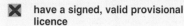
Question
To drive on the road learners MUST

Mark one answer

- ☒ have NO penalty points on their licence
- ☒ have taken professional instruction
- ☒ have a signed, valid provisional licence
- ☒ apply for a driving test within 12 months.

Answer

☒ **have a signed, valid provisional licence**

Before you drive on the road you must have a signed provisional licence in the category of vehicle that you're driving. As soon as you've received your licence, sign it. It isn't valid until you've done so.

Question
Your driving licence must be signed by

Mark one answer

- ☒ a police officer
- ☒ a driving instructor
- ☒ your next of kin
- ☒ you.

Answer

☒ **you**

Do this as soon as you receive it through the post. Don't drive until you've signed it.

Question
How long is a provisional motorcycle licence valid for?

Mark one answer

- ☒ One year.
- ☒ Two years.
- ☒ Three years.
- ☒ Five years.

Answer

☒ **Two years.**

A provisional motorcycle licence is valid for two years only. You must take and pass the theory and practical tests within two years or you'll have to wait a year before you can apply for another licence. This doesn't apply if you have a full car or moped licence.

In Northern Ireland provisional licences are valid for ten years.

Question

You are a learner motorcyclist. The law states that you can carry a passenger when

Mark one answer

☒ the motorcycle is no larger than 125cc

☒ your pillion passenger is a full licence-holder

☒ you have passed your test for a full licence

☒ you have had three years' experience of riding.

Answer

☒ you have passed your test for a full licence

When you're a learner motorcyclist you must comply with certain legal restrictions. The law states that you must

- display L plates (or D in Wales) to the front and rear on your machine
- not carry pillion passengers
- not use the motorway.

Question

What should you bring with you when taking your motorcycle test?

Mark three answers

☒ A service record book.

☒ An insurance certificate.

☒ A signed driving licence.

☒ An MOT certificate, if you haven't already sent it.

☒ A CBT certificate, if you haven't already sent it.

☒ Signed photo identity.

Answers

☒ A CBT certificate, if you haven't already sent it.

☒ A signed driving licence.

☒ Signed photo identity.

When you attend a motorcycle test your examiner will ask to see
- your driving licence
- your CBT certificate (except in Northern Ireland).

Make sure that your licence is signed and valid or your test may be cancelled. If you've already sent your CBT certificate with your test application the examiner will have a record and not need to see it again.

Question

Before taking a motorcycle test you need a

Mark one answer

☒ full moped licence

☒ full car licence

☒ Compulsory Basic Training (CBT) certificate

☒ motorcycle pass certificate.

Answer

☒ Compulsory Basic Training (CBT) certificate

You can find out about a CBT course by asking your motorcycle dealer or by telephoning 0115 901 2595.

In Northern Ireland the CBT scheme doesn't operate so all reference to CBT isn't applicable.

Question

Compulsory Basic Training (CBT) can only be carried out by

Mark one answer

☒ an Approved Driving Instructor (ADI)

☒ a road safety officer

☒ a DSA-approved training body

☒ a motorcycle main dealer.

Answer

☒ **a DSA-approved training body**

DSA approves bodies to provide training in a safe environment. Frequent checks are made to ensure a high standard of instruction. Taking a CBT course will provide you with the right start to your motorcycling life.

Question

After passing your motorcycle test you must exchange the pass certificate for a full motorcycle licence within

Mark one answer

☒ six months

☒ one year

☒ two years

☒ five years.

Answer

☒ **two years**

When you pass your practical motorcycle test you'll be issued with a pass certificate (form D.10–DL8 in Northern Ireland). You must exchange the certificate for a full licence within two years of passing your test. If you don't

- the certificate will lapse

- you'll have to retake your test if you wish to resume full motorcycle licence entitlement.

Question

For which TWO of these must you show your motor insurance certificate?

Mark two answers

☒ When you are taking your driving test.

☒ When buying or selling a vehicle.

☒ When a police officer asks you for it.

☒ When you are taxing your vehicle.

☒ When having an MOT inspection.

Answers

☒ **When a police officer asks you for it.**

☒ **When you are taxing your vehicle.**

When you take out motor insurance you'll be issued with a Certificate of Insurance. This contains details explaining who and what is insured. You'll have to produce your Certificate of Insurance when you're paying your vehicle excise duty (road tax).

If a police officer asks for your Certificate of Insurance and you don't have it with you, you may produce it at a police station within seven days (five days in Northern Ireland).

Question

For which TWO of these must you show your motorcycle insurance certificate?

Mark two answers

☒ When you are taking your motorcycle test.

☒ When buying or selling a machine.

☒ When a police officer asks you for it.

☒ When you are taxing your machine.

☒ When having an MOT inspection.

Answers

☒ When a police officer asks you for it.

☒ When you are taxing your machine.

Question

A police officer asks to see your driving documents. You do not have them with you. You may produce them at a police station within

Mark one answer

☒ five days

☒ seven days

☒ 14 days

☒ 21 days.

Answer

☒ seven days *5 days*

You don't have to carry your documents with you. If a police officer asks to see them and you don't have them with you, you may produce them at a police station within seven days (five days in Northern Ireland).

Question

Before riding anyone else's motorcycle you should make sure that

Mark one answer

☒ the machine owner has third party insurance cover

☒ your own machine has insurance cover

☒ the machine is insured for your use

☒ the owner has the insurance documents with them.

Answer

☒ the machine is insured for your use

If you borrow a motorcycle you must make sure that you're insured. Find out yourself. Don't take anyone else's word for it.

Question

Before driving anyone else's motor vehicle you should make sure that

Mark one answer

☒ the vehicle owner has third party insurance cover

☒ your own vehicle has insurance cover

☒ the vehicle is insured for your use

☒ the owner has left the insurance documents in the vehicle.

Question

What is the legal minimum insurance cover you must have to drive on public roads?

Mark one answer

☒ Third party, fire and theft.

☒ Fully comprehensive.

☒ Third party only.

☒ Personal injury cover.

Question

Your car has third party insurance. What does this cover?

Mark three answers

☒ Damage to your own car.

☒ Damage to your car by fire.

☒ Injury to another person.

☒ Damage to someone else's property.

☒ Damage to other vehicles.

☒ Injury to yourself.

Answer

☒ the vehicle is insured for your use

Don't take someone else's word on the matter. New drivers are considered a high risk and this is reflected in high insurance costs. If you're careful and don't have an accident the cost of your insurance will come down, although other factors, such as your occupation and where you live, are taken into account.

Answer

☒ Third party only.

The minimum insurance requirement by law is third party cover. This covers others involved in an accident BUT NOT damage to your vehicle. Basic third party insurance won't cover theft or fire damage. Check with your insurance company for advice on the best cover for you. Make sure that you read the policy carefully.

Answers

☒ Injury to another person.

☒ Damage to someone else's property.

☒ Damage to other vehicles.

Third party insurance doesn't cover damage to your own vehicle or injury to yourself. If you have an accident and you damage your vehicle you might have to carry out the repairs at your own expense.

Question

The cost of your insurance will be reduced if

Mark one answer

☒ your car is large and powerful

☒ you are using the car for work purposes

☒ you have penalty points on your licence

☒ you are over 25 years old.

Answer

☒ **you are over 25 years old**

Provided you haven't had previous accidents or committed any driving offences, your insurance should be less costly as you get beyond the age of 25. This is because statistics show that most accidents are caused by or involve young and/or inexperienced drivers.

NI

Question

Motor cars and motorcycles must FIRST have an MOT test certificate when they are

Mark one answer

☒ one year old

☒ three years old

☒ five years old

☒ seven years old.

Answer

☒ **three years old**

The vehicle you drive must be in good condition and roadworthy. If it's over three years old it must have a valid MOT test certificate.

In Northern Ireland a vehicle first needs an MOT test certificate when it's four years old.

Question

An MOT certificate is normally valid for

Mark one answer

☒ three years after the date it was issued

☒ 10,000 miles

☒ one year after the date it was issued

☒ 30,000 miles.

Answer

☒ **one year after the date it was issued**

Make a note of the date that your vehicle is due for an MOT. Some garages remind you, but not all of them.

NI

Question

When is it legal to drive a car over three years old without an MOT certificate?

Mark one answer

☒ Up to seven days after the old certificate has run out.

☒ When driving to an MOT centre to arrange an appointment.

☒ Just after buying a second-hand car with no MOT.

☒ When driving to an appointment at an MOT centre.

Answer

☒ **When driving to an appointment at an MOT centre.**

If a vehicle's over three years old it must have a valid MOT certificate if you want to use it on the road. The only time a vehicle's exempt is when it's being driven to an appointment at an MOT testing station.

In Northern Ireland the time limit before an MOT test is needed is four years.

Question

Your vehicle needs a current MOT certificate. You do not have one. Until you do have one you will not be able to renew your

Mark one answer

☒ driving licence

☒ vehicle insurance

☒ road tax disc

☒ vehicle registration document.

Answer

☒ **road tax disc**

You'll have to produce your MOT certificate when you renew your road tax disc (road fund licence).

Question

Which of these vehicles is not required to have an MOT certificate?

Mark two answers

☒ Police vehicle.

☒ Small trailer.

☒ Ambulance.

☒ Taxi.

☒ Caravan.

Answers

☒ **Small trailer.**

☒ **Caravan.**

Despite not needing an MOT certificate, you should ensure that your trailer is in good order and properly serviced. Tyres, wheel nuts, lights and indicators should be checked regularly.

NI

Question

Which THREE of the following do you need before you can drive legally?

Mark three answers

☒ A valid signed driving licence.

☒ A valid tax disc displayed on your vehicle.

☒ Proof of your identity.

☒ A current MOT certificate if the car is over three years old (or four years in Northern Ireland).

☒ Fully comprehensive insurance.

☒ A vehicle handbook.

Answers

☒ **A valid signed driving licence.**

☒ **A valid tax disc displayed on your vehicle.**

☒ **A current MOT certificate if the car is over three years old (or four years in Northern Ireland).**

Make sure that your vehicle's not only safe but legal.

Question
CBT completion certificates (DL196) are valid for

Mark one answer

 three years

two years

indefinitely

five years.

Answer
:x: **three years**

In order to complete the CBT course you'll have to demonstrate that you can ride confidently and safely in a variety of road and traffic conditions. Your certificate will enable you to apply for your tests. If you don't pass your tests within its three-year life you'll have to complete the CBT course again.

NI

Question
If you DO NOT pass your motorcycle tests within two years your provisional licence will expire. You can only apply for another provisional licence after

Mark one answer

three years

six months

one year

two years.

Answer
:x: **one year**

Provisional motorcycle entitlement on a provisional licence is valid for two years. If you don't pass your motorcycle test within that time the motorcycle entitlement will lapse. You can only apply for renewal of motorcycle entitlement after a period of one year.

This provision doesn't apply in Northern Ireland

Question
When you buy a motorcycle you will need a vehicle registration document from

Mark one answer

any MOT testing station

the person selling the motorcycle

your local council offices

your local trading standards officer.

Answer
:x: **the person selling the motorcycle**

You must fill in your details and send it to the Driver and Vehicle Licensing Authority (DVLA) at the address given on the document.

Question

Which THREE pieces of information are found on a vehicle registration document?

Mark three answers

- ☒ Registered keeper.
- ☒ Make of the vehicle.
- ☒ Service history details.
- ☒ Date of the MOT.
- ☒ Type of insurance cover.
- ☒ Engine size.

Answers

- ☒ Registered keeper.
- ☒ Make of the vehicle.
- ☒ Engine size.

Every vehicle used on the road has a registration document. This is issued by the Driver Vehicle Licensing Agency (DVLA) or the Driver and Vehicle Licensing Northern Ireland (DVLNI) and it keeps a record of the change of ownership. The document states

- date of first registration
- registration number
- previous keeper
- registered keeper
- make of vehicle
- engine size and chassis number
- year of manufacture
- colour.

This section looks at what to do in the event of an accident.

The questions will ask you about

- First Aid
- warning devices
- reporting procedures
- safety regulations.

Question

You are the first to arrive at the scene of an accident. Which FOUR of these should you do?

Mark four answers

☒ Leave as soon as another motorist arrives.

☒ Switch off the vehicle engine(s).

☒ Move uninjured people away from the vehicle(s).

☒ Call the emergency services.

☒ Warn other traffic.

Question

You are the first person to arrive at an accident where people are badly injured. Which THREE should you do?

Mark three answers

☒ Switch on your own hazard warning lights.

☒ Make sure that someone telephones for an ambulance.

☒ Try and get people who are injured to drink something.

☒ Move the people who are injured clear of their vehicles.

☒ Get people who are not injured clear of the scene.

Answers

☒ **Switch off the vehicle engine(s).**

☒ **Move uninjured people away from the vehicle(s).**

☒ **Call the emergency services.**

☒ **Warn other traffic.**

If you're involved in, or arrive at, the scene of an accident there are certain actions you should take. It's important to know what to do and also what NOT to do. You could save someone's life, or endanger it.

Answers

☒ **Switch on your own hazard warning lights.**

☒ **Make sure that someone telephones for an ambulance.**

☒ **Get people who are not injured clear of the scene.**

If you're the first to arrive at the scene of an accident further collisions and fire are the first concerns. Switching off vehicle engines will reduce the risk of fire.

Your hazard warning lights will let approaching traffic know that there's a need for caution.

Don't assume someone else has called the emergency services. Do it yourself.

Question

You have stopped at the scene of an accident to give help. Which THREE things should you do?

Mark three answers

☒ Keep injured people warm and comfortable.

☒ Keep injured people calm by talking to them reassuringly.

☒ Keep injured people on the move by walking them around.

☒ Give injured people a warm drink.

☒ Make sure that injured people are not left alone.

Answers

☒ **Keep injured people warm and comfortable.**

☒ **Keep injured people calm by talking to them reassuringly.**

☒ **Make sure that injured people are not left alone.**

If you stop at the scene of an accident to give help and there are casualties don't

• move injured people, unless further danger is threatened

• give the injured anything to drink.

Question

You arrive at the scene of a motorcycle accident. The rider is conscious but in shock. You should make sure that

Mark one answer

☒ the rider's helmet is removed

☒ the rider is moved to the side of the road

☒ the rider's helmet is not removed

☒ the rider is put in the recovery position.

Answer

☒ **the rider's helmet is not removed.**

At the scene of a motorcycle accident where a rider or passenger is injured

• don't remove the helmet – it could cause further injury

• offer reassurance and comfort until the emergency services arrive.

Question

You arrive at the scene of a motorcycle accident. No other vehicle is involved. The rider is unconscious, lying in the middle of the road. The first thing you should do is

Mark one answer

☒ move the rider out of the road

☒ warn other traffic

☒ clear the road of debris

☒ give the rider reassurance.

Answer

☒ **warn other traffic**

The motorcyclist is in an extremely vulnerable position, exposed to further danger from traffic. The traffic needs to slow right down and be aware of the hazard in good time.

Question

You have an accident and your pillion passenger is injured. You must NOT

Mark one answer

 reassure them

 keep them in the same position

 remove their helmet

 keep them warm.

Answer

 remove their helmet

Removing a motorcycle helmet could cause further injury. If the rider's conscious reassure them while waiting for the emergency services.

Question

A tanker is involved in an accident. Which sign would show if the tanker is carrying dangerous goods?

Mark one answer

Answer

There will be an orange label on the side and rear of the lorry. Look at this carefully and report what it says when you phone the emergency services.

Question

While driving a warning light on your vehicle's instrument panel comes on. You should

Mark one answer

☒ continue if the engine sounds alright

☒ hope that it is just a temporary electrical fault

☒ deal with the problem when there is more time

☒ check out the problem quickly and safely.

Answer

☒ **check out the problem quickly and safely**

An illuminated warning light could mean that your car is unsafe to drive. Don't take risks. If you aren't sure about the problem get a qualified mechanic to check it.

Question

For which TWO should you use hazard warning lights?

Mark two answers

☒ When you slow down quickly on a motorway because of a hazard ahead.

☒ When you have broken down.

☒ When you wish to stop on double yellow lines.

☒ When you need to park on the pavement.

Answers

☒ **When you slow down quickly on a motorway because of a hazard ahead.**

☒ **When you have broken down.**

Hazard warning lights are fitted to all modern cars and some motorcycles. They should be used to warn other road users of a hazard ahead.

Question

For which THREE should you use your hazard warning lights?

Mark three answers

☒ When you are parking in a restricted area.

☒ When you are temporarily obstructing traffic.

☒ To warn following traffic of a hazard ahead.

☒ When you have broken down.

Answers

☒ **When you are temporarily obstructing traffic.**

☒ **To warn following traffic of a hazard ahead.**

☒ **When you have broken down.**

Use them on the motorway when you have to slow down suddenly because of a queue of traffic ahead. This is to warn following traffic that you're slowing suddenly and rapidly.

Question

When are you allowed to use hazard warning lights?

Mark one answer

☒ When stopped and temporarily obstructing traffic.

☒ When driving during darkness without headlights.

☒ When parked for shopping on double yellow lines.

☒ When travelling slowly because you are lost.

Answer

☒ **When stopped and temporarily obstructing traffic.**

Don't use hazard lights

• to excuse yourself for illegal, dangerous or inconsiderate parking

• when you're moving slowly because you're lost

• when you're moving slowly due to bad weather.

Question

When should you switch on your hazard warning lights?

Mark one answer

☒ When you cannot avoid causing an obstruction.

☒ When you are driving slowly due to bad weather.

☒ When you are towing a broken down vehicle.

☒ When you are parked on double yellow lines.

Answer

☒ **When you cannot avoid causing an obstruction.**

This doesn't mean parking to shop or use a bank machine. If you need to stop for these reasons do so in an authorized parking place.

Question

You have broken down on a two-way road. You have a warning triangle. You should place the warning triangle at least how far from your vehicle?

Mark one answer

☒ 5 metres (16 feet).

☒ 25 metres (80 feet).

☒ 50 metres (165 feet).

☒ 100 metres (330 feet).

Answer

☒ **50 metres (165 feet).**

Carry an advance warning triangle in your vehicle. They fold flat and don't take up much room. Use it to warn other road users if your vehicle has broken down or there's been an accident. Place your warning triangle

• at least 50 metres (165 feet) from your vehicle on a straight, level road

• at least 150 metres (492 feet) from your vehicle on a dual carriageway or motorway.

Question

You are in an accident on an 'A' class road. You have a warning triangle with you. At what distance before the obstruction should you place the warning triangle?

Mark one answer

☒ 100 metres (330 feet).

☒ 50 metres (165 feet).

☒ 25 metres (80 feet).

☒ 150 metres (492 feet).

Question

You have broken down on an ordinary road. You have a warning triangle. It should be displayed

Mark one answer

☒ on the roof of your vehicle

☒ at least 150 metres (492 feet) behind your vehicle

☒ at least 50 metres (165 feet) behind your vehicle

☒ just behind your vehicle.

Answer

✖ **50 metres (165 feet).**

If there's a bend or hump in the road place the triangle so that approaching traffic slows down before the bend. You must give traffic enough time to react to the warning.

Use your hazard warning lights as well as a warning triangle, especially in the dark.

Answer

✖ **at least 50 metres (165 feet) behind your vehicle**

If you need to display a warning triangle make sure that it can be seen clearly by other road users. Place it on the same side of the road and clear of any obstruction.

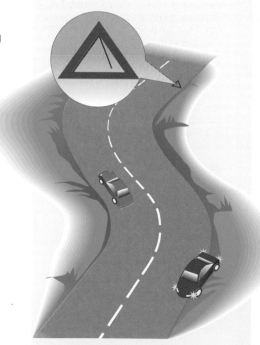

NI

Question
You are involved in a road accident with another driver. Your vehicle is damaged. Which FOUR of the following should you find out?

Mark four answers

☒ Whether the driver owns the other vehicle involved.

☒ The other driver's name, address and telephone number.

☒ The car make and registration number of the other vehicle.

☒ The occupation of the other driver.

☒ The details of the other driver's vehicle insurance.

☒ Whether the other driver is licensed to drive.

Answers

☒ **Whether the driver owns the other vehicle involved.**

☒ **The other driver's name, address and telephone number.**

☒ **The car make and registration number of the other vehicle.**

☒ **The details of the other driver's vehicle insurance.**

Try to keep calm and don't rush the proceedings. Take your time. You might be a little shaken by the incident, but try to ensure that you have all the details before you leave the scene.

Question
You have an accident while driving and someone is injured. You do not produce your insurance certificate at the time. You must report it to the police as soon as possible, or in any case within

Mark one answer

☒ 24 hours

☒ 48 hours

☒ five days

☒ seven days.

Answer

☒ **24 hours**

You must also give

• your name and address

• your vehicle owner's address

• the registration number of the vehicle

to the police, or anyone with reasonable grounds for wanting them.

In Northern Ireland accidents have to be reported to the police 'forthwith'.

Question
At a railway level crossing the red light signal continues to flash after a train has gone by. What should you do?

Mark one answer

☒ Phone the signal operator.

☒ Alert drivers behind you.

☒ Wait.

☒ Proceed with caution.

Answer

☒ **Wait.**

Don't

• proceed

• phone the signal operator immediately

• zigzag between the gates.

There may be another train coming.

Question

You break down on a level crossing. The lights have not yet begun to flash. Which THREE things should you do?

Mark three answers

☒ Telephone the signal operator.

☒ Leave your vehicle and get everyone clear.

☒ Walk down the track and signal the next train.

☒ Move the vehicle if a signal operator tells you to.

☒ Tell drivers behind what has happened.

Answers

☒ **Telephone the signal operator.**

☒ **Leave your vehicle and get everyone clear.**

☒ **Move the vehicle if a signal operator tells you to.**

Keep calm. Don't

- walk up the track to warn approaching trains
- try to restart the engine
- try to move the vehicle.

Question

You have stalled in the middle of a level crossing and cannot restart the engine. The warning bell starts to ring. You should

Mark one answer

☒ get out and clear of the crossing

☒ run down the track to warn the signalman

☒ carry on trying to restart the engine

☒ push the vehicle clear of the crossing.

Answer

☒ **get out and clear of the crossing**

Try not to panic, and stay calm, especially if you have passengers on board. If you can't restart your engine before the warning bells ring then leave the vehicle.

Question

Your vehicle has broken down on an automatic railway level crossing. What should you do FIRST?

Mark one answer

☒ Get everyone out of the vehicle and clear of the crossing.

☒ Phone the signal operator so that trains can be stopped.

☒ Walk along the track to give warning to any approaching trains.

☒ Try to push the vehicle clear of the crossing as soon as possible.

Answer

☒ **Get everyone out of the vehicle and clear of the crossing.**

Ensure that everyone is WELL clear of the crossing. In the event of an accident debris could be scattered in several directions.

Question

Your tyre bursts while you are driving. Which TWO things should you do?

Mark two answers

- ☒ Pull on the handbrake.
- ☒ Brake as quickly as possible.
- ☒ Pull up slowly at the side of the road.
- ☒ Hold the steering wheel firmly to keep control.
- ☒ Continue on at a normal speed.

Question

Which TWO things should you do when a front tyre bursts?

Mark two answers

- ☒ Apply the handbrake to stop the vehicle.
- ☒ Brake firmly and quickly.
- ☒ Let the vehicle roll to a stop.
- ☒ Hold the steering wheel lightly.
- ☒ Grip the steering wheel firmly.

Question

Your vehicle has a puncture on a motorway. What should you do?

Mark one answer

- ☒ Drive slowly to the next service area to get assistance.
- ☒ Pull up on the hard shoulder. Change the wheel as quickly as possible.
- ☒ Pull up on the hard shoulder. Use the emergency phone to get assistance.
- ☒ Switch on your hazard lights. Stop in your lane.

Question

You use the engine cut-out switch to

Mark one answer

- ☒ stop the engine in an emergency
- ☒ stop the engine for short stops
- ☒ save wear on the ignition switch
- ☒ start the engine if you lose the key.

Answers

- ☒ **Pull up slowly at the side of the road.**
- ☒ **Hold the steering wheel firmly to keep control.**

A tyre bursting can lead to a loss of control, especially if you're travelling at high speed. The correct procedure can help to stop the vehicle safely.

Answer

- ☒ **Let the vehicle roll to a stop.**
- ☒ **Grip the steering wheel firmly.**

Try not to react by applying the brakes harshly. This could lead to further loss of steering control. Indicate your intention to pull up at the side of the road and roll to a stop.

Answer

- ☒ **Pull up on the hard shoulder. Use the emergency phone to get assistance.**

Pull up on the hard shoulder and make your way to the nearest emergency telephone and request assistance. It is dangerous to try and change an offside wheel, due to fast traffic passing very close to your vehicle.

Answer

- ☒ **stop the engine in an emergency**

Most motorcycles are fitted with an engine cut-out switch. This is designed to stop the engine in an emergency and so reduce the risk of fire.

Question

On the motorway the hard shoulder should be used

Mark one answer

☒ to answer a mobile phone

☒ when an emergency arises

☒ for a short rest when tired

☒ to check a road atlas.

Answer

☒ **when an emergency arises**

Pull onto the hard shoulder and use the emergency telephone to report your problem. The telephone connects you to police control, who will put you through to an emergency breakdown service. Never cross the carriageway to use the telephone on the other side.

Question

What TWO safeguards could you take against fire risk to your vehicle?

Mark two answers

☒ Keep water levels above maximum.

☒ Carry a fire extinguisher.

☒ Avoid driving with a full tank of petrol.

☒ Use unleaded petrol.

☒ Check out any strong smell of petrol.

☒ Use low octane fuel.

Answers

☒ **Carry a fire extinguisher.**

☒ **Check out any strong smell of petrol.**

The fuel in your vehicle can be a dangerous fire hazard. Don't

• use a naked flame near the vehicle if you can smell fuel

• smoke when refuelling your vehicle.

Question

You have broken down on a motorway. When you use the emergency telephone you will be asked

Mark three answers

☒ for the number on the telephone that you are using

☒ for your driving licence details

☒ for the name of your vehicle insurance company

☒ for details of yourself and your vehicle

☒ whether you belong to a motoring organisation.

Answers

☒ **for the number on the telephone you are using**

☒ **for details of yourself and your vehicle**

☒ **whether you belong to a motoring organisation**

Have these details ready before you phone to save time. Be sure to give the correct information. For safety sake, always face the traffic when you speak on the telephone.

Question

You are on the motorway. Luggage falls from your vehicle. What should you do?

Mark one answer

☒ Stop at the next emergency telephone and contact the police.

☒ Stop on the motorway and put on hazard lights whilst you pick it up.

☒ Reverse back up the motorway to pick it up.

☒ Pull up on the hard shoulder and wave traffic down.

Answer

☒ **Stop at the next emergency telephone and contact the police.**

• Pull over onto the hard shoulder near an emergency telephone

• phone for assistance.

Don't

• stop on the carriageway

• attempt to retrieve anything.

Question
You are travelling on a motorway. A bag falls from your motorcycle. There are valuables in the bag. What should you do?

Mark one answer

☒ Go back carefully and collect the bag as quickly as possible.

☒ Stop wherever you are and pick up the bag, but only when there is a safe gap.

☒ Stop on the hard shoulder and use the emergency telephone to inform the police.

☒ Stop on the hard shoulder and then retrieve the bag yourself.

Answer

✖ **Stop on the hard shoulder and use the emergency telephone to inform the police.**

However important you think retrieving your property may be DON'T walk onto the motorway. Your bag might be creating a hazard but not as great a hazard as you would be.

Question
You are driving on a motorway. A large box falls onto the carriageway from a lorry ahead of you. The lorry does not stop. You should

Mark one answer

☒ drive to the next emergency telephone and inform the police

☒ catch up with the lorry and try to get the driver's attention

☒ stop close to the box and switch on your hazard warning lights until the police arrive

☒ pull over to the hard shoulder, then try and remove the box.

Answer

✖ **drive to the next emergency telephone and inform the police**

Lorry drivers are sometimes unaware of objects falling from their vehicles. If you see something fall off a lorry onto the motorway watch to see if the driver pulls over. If the lorry doesn't stop you should

• pull over onto the hard shoulder near an emergency telephone

• report the hazard to the police.

Question
You are driving on a motorway. When can you use hazard warning lights?

Mark two answers

☒ When a vehicle is following too closely.

☒ When you slow down quickly because of danger ahead.

☒ When you are towing another vehicle.

☒ When driving on the hard shoulder.

☒ When you have broken down, on the hard shoulder.

Answers

✖ **When you slow down quickly because of danger ahead.**

✖ **When you have broken down, on the hard shoulder.**

Hazard lights will warn the traffic travelling behind you that your vehicle is a potential hazard. Don't forget to turn them off again when you return to the carriageway or normal speed.

SECTION 14 VEHICLE LOADING

This section looks at the safety of loads.

The questions will ask you about

- vehicle loading
- stability
- towing regulations.

Question
Who is responsible for making sure that a vehicle is not overloaded?

Mark one answer

☒ The driver or rider of the vehicle.

☒ The owner of the items being carried.

☒ The person who loaded the vehicle.

☒ The owner of the vehicle.

Answer

☒ **The driver or rider of the vehicle.**

Your vehicle must not be overloaded. This will affect control and handling characteristics. If your vehicle is overloaded and it causes an accident you'll be responsible.

Question
Any load that is carried on a luggage rack MUST be

Mark one answer

☒ securely fastened when riding

☒ carried only when strictly necessary

☒ as light as possible

☒ covered with plastic sheeting.

Answer

☒ **securely fastened when riding**

Don't risk losing any luggage off your machine. It could fall into the path of following vehicles and cause danger. It's an offence to travel with an insecure load.

Question
Any load that is carried on a roof rack MUST be

Mark one answer

☒ securely fastened when driving

☒ carried only when strictly necessary

☒ as light as possible

☒ covered with plastic sheeting.

Answer

☒ **securely fastened when driving**

If you wish to carry items on the roof there are roof boxes available from automotive supply stores. These will help to keep your luggage secure and dry.

Question
When your vehicle is loaded you MUST make sure that the load will

Mark one answer

☒ remain secure

☒ be easy to unload

☒ not be damaged

☒ not damage the vehicle.

Answer

☒ **remain secure**

If the load is insecure it could become loose and fall into the path of other traffic. This could cause injury and you would be responsible.

Question
Which THREE are suitable restraints for a child under three years?

Mark three answers

☒ A child seat.

☒ An adult holding a child.

☒ An adult seat belt.

☒ A lap belt.

☒ A harness.

☒ A baby carrier.

Question
Your car is fitted with child safety door locks. When used this means that normally

Mark one answer

☒ the rear doors can only be opened from the outside

☒ the rear doors can only be opened from the inside

☒ all the doors can only be opened from the outside

☒ all the doors can only be opened from the inside.

Question
What do child locks in a vehicle do?

Mark one answer

☒ Lock the seat belt buckles in place.

☒ Lock the rear windows in the up position.

☒ Stop children from opening rear doors.

☒ Stop the rear seats from tipping forward.

Answers

☒ **A child seat.**

☒ **A harness.**

☒ **A baby carrier.**

The driver is responsible for ensuring that children under three wear suitable child restraints. If the child is in the front seat a restraint **must** be used. If the child is in the rear seat restraints **must** be used if available.

A harness or booster seat should be appropriate to the child's weight.

Answer

☒ **the rear doors can only be opened from the outside**

Safety locks prevent the doors being opened accidentally. Children travelling in the back of the car might play with the door handle, opening the door accidentally.

Answer

☒ **Stop children from opening rear doors.**

Child locks are fitted to most modern cars. They prevent the door being opened from the inside.

Question
Your vehicle is fitted with child safety door locks. You should use these so that children inside the car cannot open.

Mark one answer
- ☒ the right-hand doors
- ☒ the left-hand doors
- ☒ the rear doors
- ☒ any of the doors.

Question
Would it be safe to allow children to sit BEHIND the rear seats of a hatchback car?

Mark one answer
- ☒ Yes, if you can see clearly to the rear.
- ☒ Yes, if they're under 11 years.
- ☒ No, unless all the other seats are full.
- ☒ No, not in any circumstances.

Question
You should load a trailer so that the weight is

Mark one answer
- ☒ mostly over the nearside wheel
- ☒ evenly distributed
- ☒ mainly at the front
- ☒ mostly at the rear.

Answer
☒ **the rear doors**

If you're travelling with children in the rear seats, fitting child safety locks is a sensible safety precaution. There will be times when children are eager to get out of the car as it comes to a stop, and child safety locks will prevent them doing so until you're sure it's safe for them to do so.

Answer
☒ **No, not in any circumstances.**

Children shouldn't be allowed to sit behind the rear seats of a hatchback car. This is a crumple zone, and in a rear-end collision the bodywork may push into this area.

Answer
☒ **evenly distributed**

If you tow a trailer you need to give some thought as to how you load it. The load should be

- secured so that it can't move about while you're travelling. Movement of the load might affect steering and cause danger to other road users.
- evenly distributed.

Question

Before towing a caravan you should ensure that heavy items in it are loaded

Mark one answer

- ☒ as high as possible, mainly over the axle(s)
- ☒ as low as possible, mainly over the axle(s)
- ☒ as low as possible, forward of the axle(s)
- ☒ as high as possible, forward of the axle(s).

Answer

 as low as possible, mainly over the axle(s)

Loading like this will help the caravan to be more stable

Question

If a trailer swerves or snakes when you are towing it you should

Mark one answer

- ☒ ease off the accelerator and reduce your speed
- ☒ let go of the steering wheel and let it correct itself
- ☒ brake hard and hold the pedal down
- ☒ increase your speed as quickly as possible.

Answer

 ease off the accelerator and reduce your speed

Strong winds or buffeting from large vehicles might cause a trailer or caravan to snake or swerve. If this happens ease off the accelerator. Don't

- brake harshly
- steer sharply
- increase speed.

Question

Are passengers allowed to ride in a caravan that is being towed?

Mark one answer

- ☒ Yes.
- ☒ No.
- ☒ Only if all the seats in the towing vehicle are full.
- ☒ Only if a stabilizer is fitted.

Answer

☒ **No.**

Riding in a towed caravan is highly dangerous. The safety of the entire unit is dependent on the stability of the trailer. Moving passengers would render the caravan unstable and could cause loss of control.

Question

If a trailer swerves or snakes when you are towing it you should

Mark one answer

- [ ] ease off the throttle and reduce your speed
- [ ] let go of the handlebars and let it correct itself
- [ ] brake hard and hold the brake on
- [ ] increase your speed as quickly as possible.

Answer

✗ ease off the throttle and reduce your speed

Don't be tempted to use the steering to stop swerving or snaking. This won't help the situation. Ease off the throttle and reduce your speed.

Question

You are towing a trailer and experience snaking. How would you reduce it?

Mark one answer

- [ ] Ease off the accelerator slowly.
- [ ] Press the accelerator firmly.
- [ ] Steer sharply.
- [ ] Brake hard.

Answer

✗ Ease off the accelerator slowly.

Don't try to correct snaking or swerving by increasing your speed, braking or trying to steer against the trailer's swing.

Question

How can you stop a caravan snaking from side to side?

Mark one answer

- [ ] Turn the steering wheel slowly to each side.
- [ ] Accelerate to increase your speed.
- [ ] Stop as quickly as you can.
- [ ] Slow down very gradually.

Answer

✗ Slow down very gradually.

Keep calm and don't brake harshly or you could lose control completely.

Question

You are towing a small trailer on a busy three-lane motorway. All the lanes are open. You must

Mark two answers

☒ not exceed 60 mph

☒ not overtake

☒ have a stabilizer fitted

☒ use only the left and centre lanes.

Answers

☒ **not exceed 60 mph**

☒ **use only the left and centre lanes**

You should be aware of the speed limit for the vehicle that you're driving. Allow the faster-moving traffic to flow. Don't use the right-hand lane.

Question

You have a side-car fitted to your motorcycle. What effect will it have?

Mark one answer

☒ Reduce stability.

☒ Make steering lighter.

☒ Increase stopping distance.

☒ Increase fuel economy.

Answer

☒ **Increase stopping distance.**

If you want to fit a side-car to your motorcycle

• make sure that your machine is suitable to cope with the extra load

• make sure that the side-car is fixed correctly and properly aligned.

A side-car will affect the handling of your machine. Give yourself time to adjust to the different characteristics.

Question

A trailer on a motorcycle must be no wider than

Mark one answer

☒ 1 metre (3 feet 3 in.)

☒ ½ metre (1 foot 8 in.)

☒ 1½ metres (5 feet)

☒ 2 metres (6 feet 8 in.).

Answer

☒ **1 metre (3 feet 3 in.)**

When you're towing a trailer you must remember that you might not be able to filter through traffic. Don't 'forget' that the trailer is there.

Question
Before fitting a side-car riders must

Mark one answer

☒ have the wheels of their bike balanced

☒ have their bike's engine tuned

☒ pass the extended bike test

☒ check that their bike is suitable.

Answer

☒ **check that their bike is suitable**

Make sure that the sidecar is fixed and is properly aligned. If your machine is registered on or after 1 August 1981 the sidecar must be fitted on the left side of the machine.

Question
You want to tow a trailer behind your motorcycle. You should

Mark two answers

☒ display a 'long vehicle' sign

☒ fit a larger battery

☒ have a full motorcycle licence

☒ ensure that your engine is more than 125cc

☒ ensure that your machine has shaft drive.

Answers

☒ **have a full motorcycle licence**

☒ **ensure your engine is more than 125cc**

When you tow a trailer

• you must obey the speed limit restrictions that apply to all vehicles with trailers

• your stopping distance may be increased

• any load on the trailer must be secure

• the trailer must be fitted to the machine correctly.

Question
When may a learner motorcyclist carry a pillion passenger?

Mark one answer

☒ If the passenger holds a full licence.

☒ Not at any time.

☒ If the rider is undergoing training.

☒ If the passenger is over 21.

Answer

☒ **Not at any time.**

If you carry a pillion passenger the overall weight of riders and machine will be significantly increased compared to when riding alone.

You should have experience riding solo before carrying a passenger.

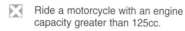

Question

Which THREE must a learner motorcyclist under 21 NOT do?

Mark three answers

- ☒ Ride a motorcycle with an engine capacity greater than 125cc.
- ☒ Pull a trailer.
- ☒ Carry a pillion passenger.
- ☒ Ride faster than 30 mph.
- ☒ Use the right-hand lane on dual carriageways.

Answers

- ☒ **Ride a motorcycle with an engine capacity greater than 125cc.**
- ☒ **Pull a trailer.**
- ☒ **Carry a pillion passenger.**

If you're a learner motorcyclist under 21 you must not ride a motorcycle on the road with an engine capacity over 125cc.

In Northern Ireland the motorcycle engine size limit for learners is 250cc.

Question

Pillion passengers MUST

Mark one answer

- ☒ have a provisional motorcycle licence
- ☒ be lighter than the rider
- ☒ wear a helmet
- ☒ wear reflective or fluorescent clothing.

Answer

- ☒ **wear a helmet**

Pillion passengers must

- sit astride the machine facing forward on a proper passenger seat
- wear a safety helmet, which is correctly fastened.

Question

Pillion passengers should

Mark one answer

- ☒ give the rider directions
- ☒ lean with the rider when going round bends and corners
- ☒ check the road behind for the rider
- ☒ give hand signals for the rider.

Answer

- ☒ **lean with the rider when going round bends and corners**

Pillion passengers should also keep both feet on the pillion footrests provided.

Question

To carry a pillión passenger your bike should have which TWO?

Mark two answers

☒ Rear footrests.

☒ An engine of 250cc or over.

☒ A top box.

☒ A grab handle.

☒ A proper passenger seat.

Answers

☒ **Rear footrests.**

☒ **A proper passenger seat.**

Pillion passengers should be instructed not to

- give hand signals
- lean away from the rider when cornering
- fidget or move around
- put their feet down to try and support the machine as you stop
- wear long, loose items that might get caught in the rear wheel or drive chain.

Conclusion

This book has been produced to help you to prepare for and pass your theory test. If you've spent sufficient time and effort you won't find the theory question paper difficult.

Passing the theory test is the first stage in becoming a safe driver or rider. Use the knowledge you've learned and put it into practice on the road. You'll never know all the answers. Throughout your driving life there will always be more to learn.

The aim of DSA is to improve road safety throughout the UK. By improving skills and knowledge we can ensure 'Safe driving for life'. This will save lives – one of them could be yours.

Service standards for theory test candidates

DSA and DVTA are committed to providing the following standards of service for test candidates.

- Theory tests will be available during weekdays, evenings and on Saturdays. A test appointment should be available for 95% of test candidates within two weeks.

- Test notification will be issued within five working days of receipt of a correctly completed application form and appropriate fee.

- 95% of telephone calls will be answered within ten seconds.

- More time may be needed to make arrangements for candidates with special needs, but a test should be available for 95% of such candidates within four weeks.

- A refund of test fees will be issued within three weeks of a valid claim with the supporting information.

- All letters, including complaints, will be answered within 15 working days.

- All candidates should be able to obtain a test booking within two months of their preferred date and time at the centre of their choice.

- No more than 0.5% of tests will be cancelled by DriveSafe Ltd (acting on behalf of DSA and DVTA).

Complaints guide for theory test candidates

DSA and DVTA aim to give their customers the best possible service. Please tell us

- when we've done well

- when you aren't satisfied.

Your comments can help us to improve the service we offer. If you have any questions about your theory test please contact 01203 662 600.

If you have any complaints about how your theory test was carried out, or any part of our customer service, please take up the matter with a member of staff if the circumstances allow. You may complete a form, available at theory test centres. Alternatively, you can write to the Head of Central Services at the following address

Head of Central Services
Driving Theory Test
PO Box 445
Coventry CV1 2ZZ
Tel: 01203 241 130
Fax: 01203 632 680

If you're dissatisfied with the reply you can write to the Managing Director at the same address.

If you're still not satisfied you can take up your complaint with

The Chief Executive
Driving Standards Agency
Stanley House
Talbot Street
Nottingham NG1 5GU

In Northern Ireland

The Chief Executive
Driver and Vehicle Licensing Agency
Balmoral Road
Belfast BT12 6QL

None of this removes your right to take your complaint to your Member of Parliament, who may decide on your case personally with the Chief Executive, the Minister, or the Parliamentary Commissioner for Administration (the Ombudsman).

Before doing this you should seek legal advice.

Compensation code for theory test candidates

DSA will normally refund the test fee, or give a free re-booking, in the following cases

- if we cancel your test
- if you cancel and give us at least three working days' notice
- if you keep the test appointment but the test doesn't take place, or isn't finished, for a reason that isn't your fault.

We'll also repay the expenses that you incurred on the day of the test because we cancelled your test at short notice. We'll consider reasonable claims for

- travelling to and from the test centre
- any pay or earnings you lost after tax (usually for half a day).

Please write to the office where you booked your test and send a receipt showing the travel costs and/or an employer's letter, which shows the earnings you lost.

DVTA has a different compensation code. If you think that you're entitled to compensation apply to the centre where you booked your test.

This compensation code doesn't affect your existing legal rights.

Theory Test Centres in Great Britain and Northern Ireland

England

Avon	Bristol		
Bedfordshire	Luton		
Berkshire	Reading	Slough	
Buckinghamshire	Milton Keynes		
Cambridgeshire	Cambridge	Peterborough	
Cheshire	Chester	Runcorn	
Cleveland	Middlesbrough		
Cornwall	Penzance	Truro	
County Durham	Durham		
Cumbria	Barrow	Carlisle	Workington
Derbyshire	Chesterfield	Derby	
Devon	Barnstaple	Exeter	Plymouth
	Torquay		
Dorset	Bournemouth	Weymouth	
East Sussex	Brighton	Eastbourne	Hastings
East Yorkshire	Hull		
Essex	Basildon	Chelmsford	Colchester
	Harlow	Southend-on-Sea	
Gloucestershire	Cheltenham	Gloucester	
Greater Manchester	Manchester	Oldham	Salford
	Stockport	Wigan	
Hampshire	Aldershot	Basingstoke	Fareham
	Portsmouth	Southampton	
Hereford and Worcester	Hereford	Worcester	
Hertfordshire	Stevenage	Watford	

Isle of Wight	Newport		
Kent	Canterbury	Gillingham	
Lancashire	Blackpool	Bolton	Preston
	Southport		
Leicestershire	Leicester		
Lincoln	Boston	Grantham	Lincoln
London - Greater	Bexley	Croydon	Ilford
	Kingston	Uxbridge	Wood Green
London - Inner	Vauxhall		
Merseyside	Birkenhead	Liverpool	St Helens
Norfolk	King's Lynn	Norwich	
North Lincolnshire	Scunthorpe		
North Yorkshire	Harrogate	Scarborough	York
North-East Lincolnshire	Grimsby		
Northamptonshire	Northampton		
Northumberland	Berwick-upon-Tweed		Morpeth
Nottinghamshire	Mansfield	Nottingham	
Oxfordshire	Oxford		
Shropshire	Shrewsbury		
Somerset	Bath	Taunton	Yeovil
South Yorkshire	Doncaster	Sheffield	
Staffordshire	Stoke-on-Trent		
Suffolk	Bury St Edmunds	Ipswich	Lowestoft
Surrey	Guildford	Staines	
Tyne and Wear	Newcastle	Sunderland	

Warwickshire	Stratford-upon-Avon		
West Midlands	Birmingham	Coventry	Dudley
	Redditch	Solihull	Sutton Coldfield
	Wolverhampton		
West Sussex	Crawley	Worthing	
West Yorkshire	Bradford	Leeds	
Wiltshire	Salisbury	Swindon	

Scotland

Borders	Galashiels		
Central	Stirling		
Dumfries and Galloway	Dumfries	Stranraer	
Fife	Dunfermline		
Grampian	Aberdeen	Elgin	Huntly
Highland	Fort William	Gairloch	Helmsdale
	Inverness	Isle of Arran	Isle of Islay
	Kyle of Lochalsh	Portree	Tongue
	Ullapool	Wick	
Lothian	Edinburgh		
Orkney	Kirkwall		
Shetland	Lerwick		
Strathclyde	Ayr	Glasgow Central	
	Glasgow North-West		Greenock
	Motherwell	Oban	Salen
	Tarbet		
Tayside	Dundee	Pitlochry	
Western Isles	Barra	Benbecula	Stornoway

Wales

Clwyd	Rhyl	
Dyfed	Aberystwyth	Haverford West
Gwent	Newport	
Gwyned	Bangor	
Mid Glamorgan	Merthyr Tydfil	
Powys	Builth Wells	
South Glamorgan	Cardiff	
West Glamorgan	Swansea	

Northern Ireland

Ballymena

Belfast

Londonderry

Newry

Omagh

Portadown

Question
When following a large vehicle you should keep well back because

Mark one answer

☒ it allows the driver to see you in his mirrors

☒ it helps the large vehicle to stop more easily

☒ it allows you to corner more quickly

☒ it helps you keep out of the wind.

Answer

❌ **it allows the driver to see you in his mirrors**

You also need to keep well back so that you get the best view of the road ahead.

Question
You wish to overtake a long, slow-moving vehicle on a busy road. You should

Mark one answer

☒ wait behind until the driver waves you past

☒ flash your headlights for the oncoming traffic to give way

☒ follow it closely and keep moving out to see the road ahead

☒ keep well back until you can see that it is clear.

Answer

❌ **keep well back until you can see that it is clear**

If you're following another vehicle that's travelling very slowly try to be patient. Keeping well back will increase your view of the road ahead. Wait until there's a safe place to overtake before you do so.

Question
In which of these situations should you avoid overtaking?

Mark one answer

☒ Just after a bend.

☒ In a one-way street.

☒ On a 30 mph road.

☒ Approaching a dip in the road.

Answer

❌ **Approaching a dip in the road.**

As you begin to think about overtaking ask yourself if it's really necessary. If you can't see well down the road stay back and wait for a safer place to pull out.

Question

You should only use a hand-held telephone when

Mark one answer

☒ your vehicle has an automatic gear change

☒ driving at low speeds

☒ you have stopped at a safe place

☒ travelling on minor roads.

Question

You are driving a vehicle fitted with a hand-held telephone. To answer the telephone you MUST

Mark one answer

☒ find a safe place to stop

☒ reduce your speed

☒ steer the car with one hand

☒ be particularly careful at junctions.

Question

On a motorcycle you can only operate a mobile telephone when

Mark two answers

☒ stationary

☒ you have a hands-free system fitted to your helmet

☒ you have a pillion passenger to help

☒ you have an automatic motorcycle

☒ you are travelling on a quiet side road.

Answer

✖ **you have stopped at a safe place**

A mobile telephone is a useful means of communication whilst away from home or the office. It can also be invaluable for use in an emergency or when you've broken down.

If you have a hand-held telephone always stop in a safe place before using it. Don't use it while moving.

Answer

✖ **find a safe place to stop**

Your attention should be on your driving at all times. If you use your telephone frequently, especially on motorways, have your vehicle fitted with a 'hands free' telephone. In each case don't let any conversation on the phone affect your concentration.

Answers

✖ **stationary**

✖ **you have a hands free system fitted to your helmet**

It's important that you're in full control of your machine at all times. If you need to use a hand-held phone you must stop at a safe place before you do so.

Question

You are driving at night and are dazzled by the headlights of an oncoming car. You should

Mark one answer

☒ slow down or stop

☒ close your eyes

☒ flash your headlights

☒ pull down the sun visor.

Question

You are riding at night and are dazzled by the headlights of an oncoming car. You should

Mark one answer

☒ slow down or stop

☒ close your eyes

☒ flash your headlight

☒ turn your head away.

Answer

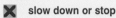 **slow down or stop**

If you're driving at night there will be extra hazards. Speeds and distances can be more difficult to judge. If the darkness makes you feel drowsy then take a rest. The lights of oncoming vehicles can often distract. If you're dazzled by them don't

• close your eyes

• flash your headlights. This will only distract the oncoming driver too.

Answer

☒ **slow down or stop**

If you're riding a motorcycle, taking a hand off the handlebars to adjust your visor might lead to loss of control. A dirty or scratched visor could cause dazzle and impair vision further.

Whether riding or driving, slow down or stop until your eyes have adjusted.

This section looks at your attitude to other road users.

The questions will ask you about

- consideration
- close following
- courtesy
- priority.

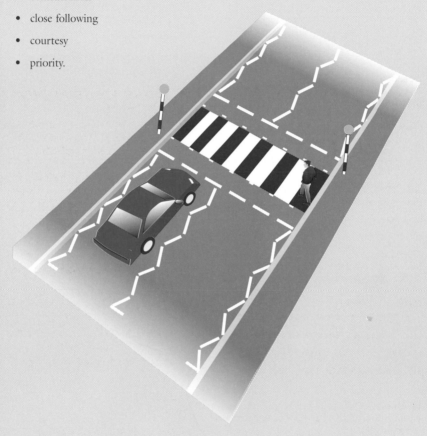

Question

A pelican crossing that crosses the road in a STRAIGHT line and has a central island MUST be treated as

Mark one answer

- [x] one crossing in daylight only
- [x] one complete crossing
- [x] two separate crossings
- [x] two crossings during darkness.

Answer

- [x] one complete crossing

The lights that control the crossing show to both directions of traffic. If a pedestrian from either side is still crossing when the amber light is flashing, you must wait.

Question

At a pelican crossing the flashing amber light means you should

Mark one answer

- [x] stop, if you can do so safely
- [x] give way to pedestrians already on the crossing
- [x] stop and wait for the green light
- [x] give way to pedestrians waiting to cross.

Answer

- [x] give way to pedestrians already on the crossing

Pelican crossings are light-controlled crossings where pedestrians use push-button controls to change the signals. Pelican crossings have no red and amber lights before green. Instead, they have a flashing amber light, which means you must give way to pedestrians on the crossing.

If it's clear you may go on.

Question

You are approaching a pelican crossing. The amber light is flashing. You must

Mark one answer

- [x] give way to pedestrians who are crossing
- [x] encourage pedestrians to cross
- [x] not move until the green light appears
- [x] stop even if the crossing is clear.

Answer

- [x] give way to pedestrians who are crossing

While the pedestrians are crossing don't

- encourage people to cross by waving or flashing your headlights – others may misunderstand your signal
- rev your engine impatiently.

Question

When should you beckon pedestrians to cross the road?

Mark one answer

- [x] At pedestrian crossings.
- [x] At no time.
- [x] At junctions.
- [x] At school crossings.

Answer

- [x] At no time.

Beckoning pedestrians to cross can be dangerous. Other road users may not have seen your signal and you might lead the pedestrians into danger.

Question

You are driving towards a zebra crossing. Pedestrians are waiting to cross. You should

Mark one answer

☒ give way to the elderly and infirm only

☒ slow down and prepare to stop

☒ use your headlamps to indicate they can cross

☒ wave at them to cross the road.

Answer

☒ **slow down and prepare to stop**

Zebra crossings have

- flashing amber beacons on both sides of the road
- black and white stripes on the crossing
- white zigzag markings on both sides of the crossing.

Where pedestrians are waiting to cross, slow down and prepare to stop.

Question

You have stopped at a pedestrian crossing. To allow pedestrians to cross you should

Mark one answer

☒ wait until they have crossed

☒ edge your vehicle forward slowly

☒ wait, revving your engine

☒ signal to pedestrians to cross.

Answer

☒ **wait until they have crossed**

Be patient, especially if they are elderly or disabled. Don't rev your engine or sound your horn.

Question

You are riding towards a zebra crossing. Pedestrians are waiting to cross. You should

Mark one answer

☒ give way to the elderly and infirm only

☒ slow down and prepare to stop

☒ use your headlamp to indicate they can cross

☒ wave at them to cross the road.

Answer

☒ **slow down and prepare to stop**

It's courteous to stop if you can do so safely, especially if

- anyone is waiting on the pavement with a pram or pushchair
- children or the elderly are hesitating to cross because of heavy traffic.

Question

You stop for pedestrians waiting to cross at a zebra crossing. They do not start to cross. What should you do?

Mark one answer

☒ Be patient and wait.

☒ Sound your horn.

☒ Drive on.

☒ Wave them to cross.

Answer

☒ **Be patient and wait.**

If you stop for pedestrians and they don't start to cross don't

- wave them across
- sound your horn.

This could be dangerous if another vehicle's approaching and hasn't seen or heard your signal.

Question
You could use the 'Two-Second Rule'

Mark one answer

☒ before restarting the engine after it's stalled

☒ to keep a safe gap from the vehicle in front

☒ before using the 'mirror, signal, manoeuvre' routine

☒ when emerging on wet roads.

Answer

☒ **to keep a safe gap from the vehicle in front**

To measure this, choose a reference point such as a bridge, sign or tree. When the vehicle ahead passes the object say to yourself 'Only a fool breaks the Two-Second Rule.' If you reach the object before you finish saying this you're TOO CLOSE.

Question
A two-second gap between yourself and the car in front is sufficient when conditions are

Mark one answer

☒ wet

☒ good

☒ damp

☒ foggy.

Answer

☒ **good**

In good, dry conditions an alert driver who's driving a vehicle with tyres and brakes in good condition needs a distance of at least two seconds from the car in front.

Question
'Tailgating' means

Mark one answer

☒ using the rear door of a hatchback car

☒ reversing into a parking space

☒ following another vehicle too closely

☒ driving with rear fog lights on.

Answer

☒ **following another vehicle too closely**

'Tailgating' is used to describe this dangerous practice, often seen in fast-moving traffic and on motorways. Following the vehicle in front too closely will

• restrict your view of the road ahead

• leave you no safety margin if the vehicle in front stops suddenly.

Question

You are driving on a clear night. There is a steady stream of oncoming traffic. The national speed limit applies. Which lights should you use?

Mark one answer

☒ Full beam headlights.

☒ Sidelights.

☒ Dipped headlights.

☒ Fog lights.

Answer

✗ **Dipped headlights.**

You should always be sure that you can be seen by other traffic. Use the main beam of your headlights only when you can be sure that you won't dazzle other traffic.

Question

Following a large goods vehicle too closely is dangerous because

Mark one answer

☒ your field of vision is seriously reduced

☒ slipstreaming will reduce wind effect

☒ your engine will overheat

☒ your brakes need a constant cooling effect.

Answer

✗ **your field of vision is seriously reduced**

Staying back will increase your view of the road ahead. This will help you to see any hazards that might occur and allow you more time to react.

Question

What is meant by 'defensive' driving?

Mark one answer

☒ Being alert and thinking ahead.

☒ Always driving slowly and gently.

☒ Always letting others go first.

☒ Pulling over for faster traffic.

Answer

✗ **Being alert and thinking ahead.**

Defensive driving is based on planning well ahead, practising effective observation and being in control. Try to be ready for any hidden hazards.

Question

You are following a vehicle on a wet road. You should leave a time gap of at least

Mark one answer

☒ one second

☒ two seconds

☒ three seconds

☒ four seconds.

Answer

✗ **four seconds**

Wet roads will increase the time it will take you to stop. The 'Two-Second Rule' will double to AT LEAST FOUR SECONDS.

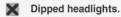

Question
While driving you approach a large puddle that's close to the left-hand kerb. Pedestrians are close to the water. You should

Mark two answers
- [ ] ignore the puddle
- [ ] brake suddenly and sound your horn
- [ ] slow down before the puddle
- [ ] try to avoid splashing the pedestrians
- [ ] wave at the pedestrians to keep back.

Answers
- [x] slow down before the puddle
- [x] try to avoid splashing the pedestrians

The effect of your vehicle driving through a puddle will be to throw water onto the pavement. If there are pedestrians close by they could be splashed by the water. Be considerate. If necessary, and it's safe to do so, avoid driving through it.

Question
You are in a line of traffic. The driver behind you is following very closely. What action should you take?

Mark one answer
- [ ] Slow down, gradually increasing the gap between you and the vehicle in front.
- [ ] Ignore the following driver and continue to drive within the speed limit.
- [ ] Signal left and wave the following driver past.
- [ ] Move out wider to a position just left of the road's centre line.

Answer
- [x] Slow down, gradually increasing the gap between you and the vehicle in front.

It can be worrying to see that the car behind is following you too closely. If you ease back from the vehicle in front you'll give yourself a greater safety margin.

Question
You are driving at the legal speed limit. A vehicle comes up quickly behind, flashing its headlamps. You should

Mark one answer
- [ ] accelerate to maintain a gap behind you
- [ ] touch the brakes to show your brake lights
- [ ] maintain your speed and prevent the vehicle from overtaking
- [ ] allow the vehicle to overtake.

Answer
- [x] allow the vehicle to overtake

Don't enforce the speed limit by blocking another vehicle's progress. This will only lead to the other driver becoming more frustrated. Slow down and allow the other vehicle to pass.

Question

When are you allowed to exceed the maximum speed limit?

Mark one answer

☒ Between midnight and 6 am.

☒ Never.

☒ When overtaking.

☒ When the road's clear.

Answer

❌ **Never.**

Speed limits are set for a reason. There are many aspects taken into consideration when the limit is set. It may depend on

- junctions
- schools
- pedestrians
- bends
- narrow roads.

Travelling at the correct speed will allow you more time to deal with potential hazards.

Question

You are driving at the legal speed limit. A vehicle behind wants to overtake. Should you try to prevent the driver overtaking?

Mark one answer

☒ No, unless it's safe to do so.

☒ Yes, because the other driver is acting dangerously.

☒ No, not at any time.

☒ Yes, because the other driver is breaking the law.

Answer

❌ **No, not at any time.**

Don't enforce the speed limit by blocking their progress. If they wish to overtake and it means they break the law, it's their risk.

Question

You are driving in traffic at the speed limit for the road. The driver behind is trying to overtake. You should

Mark one answer

☒ move closer to the car ahead, so the driver behind has no room to overtake

☒ wave the driver behind to overtake when it is safe

☒ keep a steady course and allow the driver behind to overtake

☒ accelerate to get away from the driver behind.

Answer

❌ **keep a steady course and allow the driver behind to overtake**

Keep a steady course to give the driver behind an opportunity to overtake safely. If necessary, slow down. Reacting incorrectly to another's impatience will only lead to danger.

Question
A long, heavily loaded lorry is taking a long time to overtake you. What should you do?

Mark one answer

☒ Speed up.

☒ Slow down.

☒ Hold your speed.

☒ Change direction.

Answer

☒ **Slow down.**

A long lorry with a heavy load will need more time to pass you than a car. It won't be able to accelerate to pass you quickly, especially on an uphill stretch of road. Ease off the accelerator and allow the lorry to pass.

Question
You are driving a slow-moving vehicle on a narrow road. When traffic wishes to overtake you should

Mark one answer

☒ take no action

☒ put your hazard warning lights on

☒ stop immediately and wave them on

☒ pull in safely as soon as you can do so.

Answer

☒ **pull in safely as soon as you can do so**

Try not to hold up a queue of traffic. This might lead to other road users becoming impatient. If you're driving a slow-moving vehicle and the road is narrow look out for a safe place to pull in.

Question
You are driving a slow-moving vehicle on a narrow winding road. You should

Mark one answer

☒ keep well out to stop vehicles overtaking dangerously

☒ wave following vehicles past you if you think they can overtake quickly

☒ pull in safely when you can, to let following vehicles overtake

☒ give a left signal when it is safe for vehicles to overtake you.

Answer

☒ **pull in safely when you can, to let following vehicles overtake**

Don't

- wave the other traffic on – they may not have seen your signal
- show discourtesy by not pulling in at a safe place.

Try to be courteous and considerate to other road users. Imagine how you would feel if you were the following driver or rider.

Question
You are riding a motorcycle and following a large vehicle at 40 mph. You should position yourself

Mark one answer

☒ close behind to make it easier to overtake the vehicle

☒ to the left of the road to make it easier to be seen

☒ close behind the vehicle to keep out of the wind

☒ well back so that you can see past the vehicle.

Answer

☒ **well back so that you can see past the vehicle**

You need to be able to see well down the road and be ready for any hazards that occur. Staying too close to the vehicle will leave you insufficient separation distance and also reduce your view of the road ahead.

Question
Which THREE of the following emergency vehicles will use blue flashing beacons?

Mark three answers

☒ Motorway maintenance.

☒ Bomb disposal team.

☒ Blood transfusion.

☒ Police vehicle.

☒ Breakdown recovery vehicle.

Answer

☒ **Bomb disposal team.**

☒ **Blood transfusion.**

☒ **Police vehicle.**

Try to move out of the way of emergency vehicles with blue flashing beacons. Do so safely and without delay.

Question
Which THREE of these emergency services might have blue flashing beacons?

Mark three answers

☒ Coastguard.

☒ Bomb disposal team.

☒ Gritting lorries.

☒ Animal ambulances.

☒ Mountain rescue.

☒ Doctors' cars.

Answer

☒ **Coastguard.**

☒ **Bomb disposal team.**

 ☒ **Mountain rescue.**

Question
What type of emergency vehicle is fitted with a green flashing light?

Mark one answer
- ☒ Fire engine.
- ☒ Road gritter.
- ☒ Ambulance.
- ☒ Doctor's car.

Answer
☒ Doctor's car.

A green flashing light on a vehicle means the driver or passenger is a doctor on an emergency call. Give way to them if it's safe to do so. Be aware that the vehicle may be travelling quickly or may stop in a hurry.

Question
A flashing green beacon on a vehicle means

Mark one answer
- ☒ police on non-urgent duties
- ☒ doctor on an emergency call
- ☒ road safety patrol operating
- ☒ gritting in progress.

Answer
☒ doctor on emergency call

If you see such a vehicle in your mirrors allow it to pass if you can. Be aware that someone's life could depend on the driver making good progress through traffic.

Question
A vehicle has a flashing green light. What does this mean?

Mark one answer
- ☒ A doctor is answering an emergency call.
- ☒ The vehicle is slow-moving.
- ☒ It is a motorway police patrol vehicle.
- ☒ A vehicle is carrying hazardous chemicals.

Answer
☒ A doctor is answering an emergency call.

A doctor attending an emergency might show a green flashing light on his or her vehicle. Give way to them as they will need to reach their destination quickly. Be aware that they might pull over suddenly.

Question
Diamond-shaped signs give instructions to

Mark one answer
- ☒ tram drivers
- ☒ bus drivers
- ☒ lorry drivers
- ☒ taxi drivers.

Answer
☒ tram drivers

These signs that apply to trams only. They're are directed at tram drivers but you should know their meaning so that you're aware of the priorities and are able to anticipate the actions of the driver.

Question

A bus is stopped at a bus stop ahead of you. Its right-hand indicator is flashing. You should

Mark one answer

☒ flash your headlights and slow down

☒ slow down and give way if it is safe to do so

☒ sound your horn and keep going

☒ slow down and then sound your horn.

Answer

☒ **slow down and give way if it is safe to do so**

Give way to buses whenever you can do so safely, especially when they signal to pull away from bus stops. Look out for people leaving the bus and crossing the road. Don't

- flash your headlights
- sound your horn
- give any other misleading signal.

Question

You should ONLY flash your headlamps to other road users

Mark one answer

☒ to show that you are giving way

☒ to show that you are about to reverse

☒ to tell them that you have right of way

☒ to let them know that you're there.

Answer

☒ **to let them know that you're there**

You should only flash your headlamps to warn others of your presence. Don't use them to

- greet others
- show impatience
- give up your priority.

Question

What should you use your horn for?

Mark one answer

☒ To alert others to your presence.

☒ To claim your right of way.

☒ To greet other road users.

☒ To signal your annoyance.

Answer

☒ **To alert others to your presence.**

Don't use it to

- greet others
- show impatience
- give priority.

Your horn shouldn't be used between 11.30 pm and 7 am in a built-up area or when your vehicle's stationary – unless a moving vehicle poses a danger.

Question

A vehicle pulls out in front of you at a junction. What should you do?

Mark one answer

☒ Swerve past it and blow your horn.

☒ Flash your headlights and drive up close behind.

☒ Slow down and be ready to stop.

☒ Accelerate past it immediately.

Answer

☒ **Slow down and be ready to stop.**

Try to be ready for the unexpected. Plan ahead and learn to anticipate hazards. You'll then give yourself more time to react to any problems that might occur.

Be tolerant of the behaviour of other road users who don't behave correctly.

Question

When riding a motorcycle your normal road position should allow you to

Mark two answers

☒ be seen by traffic ahead emerging from junctions

☒ be seen in the mirrors of the vehicle in front

☒ hold back vehicles wishing to overtake

☒ let other vehicles overtake on the left

☒ remain within ½ metre (1.5 feet) from the kerb.

Answer

☒ **be seen by traffic ahead emerging from junctions**

☒ **be seen in the mirrors of the vehicle in front**

Keep clear of the centre of the road. You might

• obstruct overtaking traffic

• put yourself in danger from oncoming traffic

• encourage other traffic to overtake you on the left.

Question

You are in a one-way street and want to turn right. You should position yourself

Mark one answer

☒ in the right-hand lane

☒ in the left-hand lane

☒ in either lane, depending on the traffic

☒ just left of the centre line.

Answer

☒ **in the right-hand lane**

If you're travelling in a one-way street and wish to turn right you should take up a position in the right-hand lane. This will enable other road users not wishing to turn to proceed on the left. Indicate your intention and take up your position in good time.

Question

You wish to turn right ahead. Why should you take up the correct position in good time?

Mark one answer

☒ To allow other drivers to pull out in front of you.

☒ To give a better view into the road that you're joining.

☒ To help other road users know what you intend to do.

☒ To allow drivers to pass you on the right.

Answer

☒ **To help other road users know what you intend to do.**

If you wish to turn right into a side road take up your position in good time. Move to the centre of the road when it's safe to do so. This will allow vehicles to pass you on the left. Early planning will show other traffic what you intend to do.

This section looks at safety and your vehicle.

The questions will ask you about

- fault detection
- defects and their effect on safety
- use of safety equipment
- emissions
- noise.

Question
Which of these, if allowed to get low, could cause an accident?

Mark one answer

☒ Antifreeze level.

☒ Brake fluid level.

☒ Battery water level.

☒ Radiator coolant level.

Answer

☒ **Brake fluid level.**

In order to keep your vehicle in good working order you should carry out frequent checks. As a driver or rider you must ensure that you're using a safe vehicle or machine that won't endanger other road users.

Question
Which FOUR of these **must** be in good working order for your car to be roadworthy?

Mark four answers

☒ Temperature gauge.

☒ Speedometer.

☒ Windscreen washers.

☒ Windscreen wipers.

☒ Oil warning light.

☒ Horn.

Answers

☒ **Speedometer.**

☒ **Windscreen washers.**

☒ **Windscreen wipers.**

☒ **Horn.**

Also check the

- lights – get someone to help you check the brake lights
- indicators
- battery – this may be maintenance-free and not need topping up
- steering – check for 'play' in the steering
- oil
- water
- suspension.

Question
A loose drive chain on a motorcycle could cause

Mark one answer

☒ the front wheel to wobble

☒ the ignition to cut out

☒ the brakes to fail

☒ the rear wheel to lock.

Answer

☒ **the rear wheel to lock**

Drive chains are subject to wear and require frequent adjustment and lubrication. If the chain is worn or slack it can jump off the sprocket and lock the rear wheel.

Question

Which THREE does the law require you to keep in good condition?

Mark three answers

☒ Gears.

☒ Clutch.

☒ Headlights.

☒ Windscreen.

☒ Seat belts.

Answers

☒ **Headlights.**

☒ **Windscreen.**

☒ **Seat belts.**

Also check the

- lights – get someone to help you check the brake lights

- indicators

- battery – this may be maintenance-free and not need topping up

- steering – check for 'play' in the steering

- oil

- water

- suspension.

Whether driving or riding, check that the speedometer is working once you've moved off.

Question

New petrol-engined cars must be fitted with catalytic converters. The reason for this is to

Mark one answer

☒ control exhaust noise levels

☒ prolong the life of the exhaust system

☒ allow the exhaust system to be recycled

☒ reduce harmful exhaust emissions.

Answer

☒ **reduce harmful exhaust emissions**

We should all be concerned by the effect traffic has on our environment. Fumes from vehicles are causing damage to the air around us. Catalytic converters act like a filter, removing some of the toxic waste.

Question

Which TWO are badly affected if the tyres are under-inflated?

Mark two answers

☒ Braking.

☒ Steering.

☒ Changing gear.

☒ Parking.

Answers

☒ **Braking.**

☒ **Steering.**

Your tyres are your only grip on the road and therefore very important to your safety.

Incorrect tyre pressures will affect steering and braking so it's very important that you take the time to attend to them. Correct tyre pressures can reduce the risk of skidding and will provide a more comfortable ride.

Question
What can cause heavy steering?

Mark one answer
☒ Driving on ice.
☒ Badly worn brakes.
☒ Over-inflated tyres.
☒ Under-inflated tyres.

Answer
☒ **Under-inflated tyres.**

If your tyres don't have enough air in them they'll drag against the surface of the road. This makes the steering feel heavy.

Question
It is essential that tyre pressures are checked regularly. When should this be done?

Mark one answer
☒ After any lengthy journey.
☒ After driving at high speed.
☒ When tyres are hot.
☒ When tyres are cold.

Answer
☒ **When tyres are cold.**

When you check the tyre pressures do so when the tyres are cold. This will give you a more accurate reading. The heat generated from a long journey will raise the pressure inside the tyre.

Question
How often should motorcycle tyre pressures be checked?

Mark one answer
☒ Only during each regular service.
☒ After each long journey.
☒ At least monthly.
☒ At least weekly.

Answer
☒ **At least weekly.**

As a motorcyclist your tyres are vital to your safety. Make sure that you check the pressure in your tyres at least once a week. Don't ride your machine if the tyres are incorrectly inflated.

Question
It is important that tyre pressures are correct. They should be checked at least

Mark one answer
☒ once a week
☒ every time the vehicle is serviced
☒ every four weeks
☒ every time the vehicle has an MOT test.

Answer
☒ **once a week**

Regular checks of the pressure will also highlight any tyre wear or damage.

Question

Why should tyres be kept to the pressure the manufacturer tells you?

Mark one answer

☒ To keep the car the right height off the road.

☒ To save wear on the engine.

☒ To stop the car from sloping to one side.

☒ To help prevent the car from skidding.

Answer

✖ **To help prevent the car from skidding.**

If you aren't sure of the correct tyre pressures, check the vehicle handbook. If you don't have a handbook, go to a garage where a chart showing the correct pressures is displayed. Incorrect tyre pressures will affect steering and braking so it's very important to take the time to ensure that they're correct.

Question

Driving with under-inflated tyres can affect

Mark two answers

☒ engine temperature

☒ fuel consumption

☒ braking

☒ oil pressure.

Answers

✖ **fuel consumption**

✖ **braking**

Regular checks of tyre pressures can prevent these effects.

Question

What is the most important factor in avoiding running into the car in front?

Mark one answer

☒ Making sure your brakes are efficient.

☒ Always driving at a steady speed.

☒ Keeping the correct separation distance.

☒ Having tyres that meet the legal requirements.

Answer

✖ **Keeping the correct separation distance.**

Having tyres in a good condition and at the correct pressure won't take away all the risks when driving or riding. Leaving a correct separation distance and planning well ahead will help to make you a safer driver.

Question

The legal minimum depth of tread for car tyres over three-quarters of the breadth is

Mark one answer

☒ 2.5 mm

☒ 4 mm

☒ 1 mm

☒ 1.6 mm.

Answer

✖ **1.6 mm**

Tyres must have a good depth of tread. The legal limit for cars is a minimum of 1.6 mm. This depth should be throughout the central three-quarters of the breadth of the tyre and around the entire circumference.

Question
The legal minimum depth of tread for motorcycle tyres is

Mark one answer

☒ 2.5 mm

☒ 4 mm

☒ 1 mm

☒ 1.6 mm.

Answer

☒ 1 mm

The entire original tread should be continuous. Don't ride a machine with worn tyres.

Your tyres are your only contact with the road so it's very important that you ensure they're in good condition.

Question
Your motorcycle has tubed tyres fitted as standard. When replacing a tyre you should

Mark one answer

☒ replace the tube if it is 6 months old

☒ replace the tube if it has covered 6,000 miles

☒ replace the tube only if replacing the rear tyre

☒ replace the tube with each change of tyre.

Answer

☒ **replace the tube with each change of tyre**

It isn't worth taking risks to save money. Your life could depend on the condition of your machine.

Question
You are riding a machine of more than 50cc. Which FOUR would make a tyre illegal?

Mark four answers

☒ Tread less than 1.6 mm deep.

☒ Tread less than 1 mm deep.

☒ A large bulge in the wall.

☒ A recut tread.

☒ Exposed ply or cord.

☒ A stone wedged in the tread.

Answers

☒ **Tread less than 1 mm deep.**

☒ **A large bulge in the wall.**

☒ **A recut tread.**

☒ **Exposed ply or cord.**

When checking tyres make sure there are no bulges or cuts in the side walls. Always buy your tyres from a reputable dealer to ensure quality and value for money.

Question

It is illegal to drive with tyres that

Mark one answer

☒ have a large deep cut in the side wall

☒ have been bought second-hand

☒ are of different makes

☒ have painted walls.

Answer

❌ **have a large deep cut in the side wall**

When checking your tyres for cuts and bulges in the side walls don't forget the inner walls (i.e., those facing each other under the vehicle).

Question

Excessive or uneven tyre wear can be caused by faults in the

Mark two answers

☒ braking system

☒ suspension

☒ gearbox

☒ exhaust system.

Answers

❌ **braking system**

❌ **suspension**

Uneven wear on your tyres can be caused by the condition of your vehicle. Have it serviced regularly so that the brakes, steering and wheel alignment are checked.

Question

Your vehicle pulls to one side when braking. You should

Mark one answer

☒ change the tyres around

☒ consult your garage as soon as possible

☒ pump the pedal when braking

☒ use your handbrake at the same time.

Answer

❌ **consult your garage as soon as possible**

The brakes on your vehicle or machine must be effective and properly adjusted. If your vehicle pulls to one side when braking take it to be checked by a qualified mechanic. Don't take risks.

Question

The main cause of brake fade is

Mark one answer

☒ the brakes overheating

☒ air in the brake fluid

☒ oil on the brakes

☒ the brakes out of adjustment.

Answer

❌ **the brakes overheating**

If your vehicle is fitted with drum brakes they can get hot and may lose a lot of their effect. This happens when they're continually used, such as on a long, steep downhill stretch of road. Using a lower gear will assist the braking and prevent the vehicle gaining momentum.

Question

If you notice a strong smell of petrol as you drive along you should

Mark one answer

- ☒ not worry, as it is only exhaust fumes
- ☒ carry on at a reduced speed
- ☒ expect it to stop in a few miles
- ☒ stop and investigate the problem.

Answer

☒ **stop and investigate the problem**

Don't smoke or put naked lights anywhere near the leakage. Have it checked by a qualified mechanic as soon as possible. Your vehicle could be a fire hazard.

Question

When are you allowed to drive if your brake lights DO NOT work?

Mark one answer

- ☒ During the daytime.
- ☒ When going for an MOT test.
- ☒ At no time.
- ☒ In an emergency.

Answer

☒ **At no time.**

Before you drive or ride you must ensure that all your lights are in good working order. All lights on your vehicle must be capable of working whether it's day or night. Get someone to help you check the brake lights. Don't drive if they aren't working.

Question

When may you use hazard warning lights?

Mark one answer

- ☒ To park alongside another car.
- ☒ To park on double yellow lines.
- ☒ When you are being towed.
- ☒ When you have broken down.

Answer

☒ **When you have broken down.**

Hazard warning lights may be used to warn other road users when you

- have broken down and are causing an obstruction
- are on a motorway and want to warn the traffic behind you of a hazard ahead.

Don't use them

- when being towed
- when stopped in a restricted area, unless you're causing a hazard.

Question

Hazard warning lights should be used when vehicles are

Mark one answer

- ☒ broken down and causing an obstruction
- ☒ faulty and moving slowly
- ☒ being towed along a road
- ☒ reversing into a side road.

Answer

☒ **broken down and causing an obstruction**

Don't use hazard lights as an excuse for illegal parking. If you do use them don't forget to switch them off when you move away. There must be a warning light on the control panel to show when the hazard lights are in operation.

Question

Why is it important that footwear is suitable for driving?

Mark one answer

- [ ] To help you adjust your seat.
- [ ] To enable you to walk for assistance should you need to.
- [ ] To maintain control of the pedals.
- [ ] To prevent wear on the pedals.

Answer

☒ **To maintain control of the pedals.**

Question

It is important to wear suitable shoes when you're driving. Why is this?

Mark one answer

- [ ] To prevent wear on the pedals.
- [ ] To maintain control of the pedals.
- [ ] To enable you to adjust your seat.
- [ ] To enable you to walk for assistance if you break down.

Answer

☒ **To maintain control of the pedals.**

When you're driving or riding ensure that you're wearing comfortable clothing. Comfortable shoes will ensure that you have proper control over the foot pedals.

Question

A properly adjusted head restraint will

Mark one answer

- [ ] make you more comfortable
- [ ] help you to avoid neck injury
- [ ] help you to relax
- [ ] help you to maintain your driving position.

Answer

☒ **help you to avoid neck injury**

The restraint should be adjusted so that it gives maximum protection to the head. This will help in the event of a rear-end collision.

Question

What will reduce the risk of neck injury resulting from a collision?

Mark one answer

- [ ] An air-sprung seat.
- [ ] Anti-lock brakes.
- [ ] A collapsible steering wheel.
- [ ] A properly adjusted head restraint.

Answer

☒ **A properly adjusted head restraint.**

Head restraints will reduce the risk of neck injury if you're involved in a collision. They must be properly adjusted. Make sure they aren't positioned too low, as in an accident they could cause damage to the neck.

Question
Which of the following WOULD NOT make you more visible in daylight?

Mark one answer

☒ A black helmet.

☒ A white helmet.

☒ Switching on your dipped headlamp.

☒ Wearing a fluorescent jacket.

Answer

☒ **A black helmet.**

Wearing bright or fluorescent clothes will help other road users to see you. Wearing a white helmet can also make you more visible.

Question
You are riding a motorcycle in very hot weather. You should

Mark one answer

☒ ride with your visor fully open

☒ continue to wear protective clothing

☒ wear trainers instead of boots

☒ slacken your helmet strap.

Answer

☒ **continue to wear protective clothing**

In very hot weather it's tempting to ride in light summer clothes. Don't do this. If you fall from your machine you'll have no protection from the hard road surface. Always wear your protective clothing, whatever the weather.

Question
Why should you wear fluorescent clothing when riding in daylight?

Mark one answer

☒ It reduces wind resistance.

☒ It prevents injury if you come off the machine.

☒ It helps other road users to see you.

☒ It keeps you cool in hot weather.

Answer

☒ **It helps other road users to see you.**

When riding a motorcycle it's very important that other road users are able to see you clearly. Fluorescent clothing will help towards this, reducing the risk of an accident. You must be visible from all sides.

Reflective strips

Reflective patches

Question

Which of the following makes it easier for motorcyclists to be seen?

Mark three answers

☒ Using dipped headlights.

☒ A fluorescent jacket.

☒ A white helmet.

☒ A grey helmet.

☒ Black leathers.

☒ A tinted visor.

Question

You are carrying two children and their parents in your car. Who is responsible for seeing that the children wear seat belts?

Mark one answer

☒ The children's parents.

☒ You.

☒ The front-seat passenger.

☒ The children.

Answers

☒ **Using dipped headlights.**

☒ **A fluorescent jacket.**

☒ **A white helmet.**

Many road accidents involving motorcyclists occur because another road user didn't see them. Using some form of visibility aid will help others to see you. Be aware that you're vulnerable and ride defensively.

Answer

☒ **You.**

Seat belts save lives and reduce the risk of injury. You MUST wear a seat belt unless you're exempt. There are also legal requirements for your passengers. Make sure that you know the rules for wearing seat belts. Check the chart below.

	FRONT SEAT	REAR SEAT	RESPONSIBILITY
Driver	Seat belt must be worn if fitted		Driver
Child under 3 years	Appropriate child restraint must be worn	Appropriate child restraint must be worn if available	Driver
Child aged 3 to 11 and under 1.5 metres (about 5 feet)	Appropriate child restraint must be worn if available. If not, an adult seat belt must be worn.	Appropriate child restraint must be worn if available. If not, an adult seat belt must be worn if available.	Driver
Child aged 12 or 13 or a younger child 1.5 metres in height (about 5 feet) or more	Adult seat belt must be worn if available	Adult seat belt must be worn if available	Driver
Adult passengers	Seat belt must be worn if available	Seat belt must be worn if available	Passenger

Question

Car passengers MUST wear a seat belt if one is available, unless they are

Mark one answer

☒ under 14 years old

☒ under 1.5 metres (5 feet) in height

☒ sitting in the rear seat

☒ exempt for medical reasons.

Answer

☒ **exempt for medical reasons**

Although it's your adult passengers' responsibility for wearing a seat belt, remind them to put them on as they get in the car.

Question

A car driver MUST ensure that seat belts are worn by

Mark one answer

☒ all front-seat passengers

☒ all passengers

☒ all rear-seat passengers

☒ children under 14.

Answer

☒ **children under 14**

Study the chart regarding seat belts. You could be responsible for your passenger wearing the appropriate restraint.

Question

Which of the following fairings would give you the best weather protection?

Mark one answer

☒ Handlebar.

☒ Sports.

☒ Touring.

☒ Windscreen.

Answer

☒ **Touring.**

Fairings give protection to the hands, legs and feet. They also make riding more comfortable by keeping you out of the wind.

Question
Your safety helmet has a small crack. You should

Mark one answer
- [ ] get a new one before riding
- [ ] ride at low speeds only
- [ ] ask the police to inspect it
- [ ] have it repaired by an expert.

Answer
✗ get a new one before riding

If you damage your motorcycle helmet, even slightly, buy a new one. The smallest damage can make a helmet unreliable. A little expense now may save your life later.

Buy a white helmet if possible. They're much more easily seen by other road users.

Question
Your visor becomes badly scratched. You should

Mark one answer
- [ ] polish it with a fine abrasive
- [ ] replace it
- [ ] wash it in soapy water
- [ ] clean it with petrol.

Answer
✗ replace it

Your visor protects your eyes from wind, rain, insects and road dirt. It's therefore important to keep it clean and in good repair. A badly scratched visor might

- obscure your view
- cause dazzle from lights of oncoming vehicles.

Question
When riding on public roads a motorcyclist's visor or goggles must display which Kite mark?

Answer
✗ BSI.

A visor or goggles are vital to protect your eyes from wind, rain, insects and road dirt. Make sure that yours comply with the British Standard Institute and have the mark to show that they do.

Mark one answer
- [ ] ACU.
- [ ] BMF.
- [ ] MAG.
- [ ] BSI.

Question

You are testing your suspension. You notice that your vehicle keeps bouncing when you press down on the front wing. What does this mean?

Mark one answer

☒ Worn tyres.

☒ Tyres under-inflated.

☒ Steering wheel not located centrally.

☒ Worn shock absorbers.

Answer

✖ **Worn shock absorbers.**

If you find that your vehicle bounces as you drive around a corner or bend the shock absorbers might be worn. Press down on the front wing and if the vehicle continues to bounce take it to be checked by a qualified mechanic.

Question

In which of these containers may you carry petrol in a motor vehicle?

A   B

C   D

Mark one answer

☒ A.

☒ B.

☒ C.

☒ D.

Answer

✖ **A.**

Petrol may be carried in your vehicle but it must be carried in a container designed for that purpose. Don't use other types as these might leak or perish. Suitable containers are available in most motor shops and petrol stations.

Question

You must NOT sound your horn

Mark one answer

☒ between 10 pm and 6 am in a built-up area

☒ at any time in a built-up area

☒ between 11.30 pm and 7 am in a built-up area

☒ between 11.30 pm and 6 am on any road.

Answer

✖ **between 11.30 pm and 7 am in a built-up area**

Vehicles can be noisy. Every effort must be made to prevent excessive noise, especially in built-up areas at night. Don't

- rev the engine
- sound the horn between 11.30 pm and 7 am (unless it's necessary to warn a moving vehicle).

Question
When should you NOT use your horn in a built-up area?

Mark one answer

☒ Between 8 pm and 8 am.

☒ Between 9 pm and dawn.

☒ Between dusk and 8 am.

☒ Between 11.30 pm and 7 am.

Answer
☒ **Between 11.30 pm and 7 am.**

Flash your headlights as an alternative. Only sound your horn to prevent an accident.

Question
You cannot see clearly behind when reversing. What should you do?

Mark one answer

☒ Open your window to look behind.

☒ Open the door and look behind.

☒ Look in the nearside mirror.

☒ Ask someone to guide you.

Answer
☒ **Ask someone to guide you.**

If you want to turn your car around try to find a place where you have good all-round vision. If this isn't possible and you're unable to see clearly then get someone to guide you.

Question
When must you use a dipped headlight during the day?

Mark one answer

☒ On country roads.

☒ Along narrow streets.

☒ In poor visibility.

☒ When parking.

Answer
☒ **In poor visibility.**

It's important that other road users can see you clearly at all times. It will help other road users to see you if you use dipped headlights during the day. If there's limited visibility you MUST use them.

Question
Your side stand is not raised fully when you start to ride. What could this do?

Mark one answer

☒ Alter the machine's centre of gravity.

☒ Catch on your feet.

☒ Dig into the ground when you are cornering.

☒ Cause the machine to steer badly.

Question
What will cause high fuel consumption?

Mark one answer

☒ Poor steering control.

☒ Accelerating around bends.

☒ Driving in high gears.

☒ Harsh braking and accelerating.

Question
When driving a car fitted with automatic transmission what would you use 'kick down' for?

Mark one answer

☒ Cruise control.

☒ Quick acceleration.

☒ Slow braking.

☒ Fuel economy.

Answer

☒ **Dig into the ground when you are cornering.**

Make sure that your side stand's fully up before you move off. If it isn't up it could dig into the ground as you move away and might lead to an accident.

Answer

☒ **Harsh braking and accelerating.**

Look after your vehicle or machine. Have it regulary serviced and keep all the lights and windows (on a vehicle) clean. Driving or riding 'sympathetically' will help you to keep fuel consumption down. This practice is kinder to the environment and will also save you money.

Answer

☒ **Quick acceleration.**

'Kick down' selects a lower gear, enabling the vehicle to accelerate faster.

This section looks at safety margins and how they can be affected by conditions.

The questions will ask you about

- stopping distances
- road surfaces
- skidding
- weather conditions.

Question
Stopping in good conditions at 30 mph takes at least

Mark one answer
☒ two car lengths
☒ six car lengths
☒ three car lengths
☒ one car length.

Answer
☒ **six car lengths**

It's very important that you know your overall stopping distance at all speeds. Stopping distances increase dramatically as road speed increases. Knowing your stopping distance will reduce the risk of an accident as you'll know how much room you need to leave between you and the vehicle in front.

Question
You are on a good, dry road surface and in a vehicle with good brakes and tyres. What is the shortest overall stopping distance at 40 mph?

Mark one answer
☒ 23 metres (75 feet).
☒ 96 metres (315 feet).
☒ 53 metres (175 feet).
☒ 36 metres (120 feet).

Answer
☒ **36 metres (120 feet).**

Factors that affect how long it takes you to stop include

* how fast you're going
* whether you're travelling on the level, uphill or downhill
* the weather and road conditions
* the condition of tyres, brakes and suspension
* your reaction times.

Question
What is the braking distance at 50 mph?

Mark one answer
☒ 55 metres (180 feet).
☒ 24 metres (79 feet).
☒ 14 metres (45 feet).
☒ 38 metres (125 feet).

Answer
☒ **38 metres (125 feet).**

The braking distance is how far you travel from the moment you first apply the brakes to the point where you stop.

Stopping distance can be divided into
* thinking distance
* braking distance.

The thinking distance is how far you travel from the moment you see the **need** to brake to the moment you **apply** the brakes.

Question
You are riding a motorcycle in good road conditions. The most effective way to use the brakes is to

Mark one answer

☒ apply both brakes with greater pressure on the rear

☒ apply both brakes with equal pressure

☒ apply the rear brake first and the front just before you stop

☒ apply both brakes with greater pressure on the front.

Answer

☒ **apply both brakes with greater pressure on the front**

This technique gives the best stopping power in good conditions because

- the combined weight of the machine and rider is thrown forward

- the front tyre is pressed more firmly on the road, giving a better grip.

Question
What is the shortest stopping distance at 70 mph?

Mark one answer

☒ 53 metres (175 feet).

☒ 60 metres (200 feet).

☒ 73 metres (240 feet).

☒ 96 metres (315 feet).

Answer

☒ **96 metres (315 feet).**

Note that this is the shortest distance. It will take **at least** this distance to think, brake and stop.

At 30 mph

Thinking distance	Braking distance	Overall stopping distance
9m (30ft)	14m (45ft)	23m (75ft)

At 50 mph

Thinking distance	Braking distance	Overall stopping distance
15m (50ft)	38m (125ft)	53m (175ft)

At 70 mph

Thinking distance	Braking distance	Overall stopping distance
21m (70ft)	75m (245ft)	96m (315ft)

Question

You are driving at 50 mph in good conditions. What would be your shortest stopping distance?

Mark one answer

☒ 23 metres (75 feet).

☒ 36 metres (120 feet).

☒ 53 metres (175 feet).

☒ 73 metres (240 feet).

Answer

☒ **53 metres (175 feet).**

Stopping distances can be difficult to visualise. Try thinking in terms that mean something to you. This could be

- car or motorcycle lengths
- the 100 metre sprint
- the length of a football pitch (which is about 100 metres/330 feet).

Question

You are travelling at 50 mph on a good, dry road. What is your overall stopping distance?

Mark one answer

☒ 36 metres (120 feet).

☒ 53 metres (175 feet).

☒ 75 metres (245 feet).

☒ 96 metres (315 feet).

Answer

☒ **53 metres (175 feet).**

Even in good conditions it will take you further than you think for your car to stop. Don't just learn the figures – **understand** how far the distance is.

Question

What is the shortest overall stopping distance on a dry road from 60 mph?

Mark one answer

☒ 53 metres (175 feet).

☒ 58 metres (190 feet).

☒ 73 metres (240 feet).

☒ 96 metres (315 feet).

Answer

☒ **73 metres (240 feet).**

Pace out 73 metres and then look back. It's probably further than you think.

Question

You are on a fast, open road in good conditions. For safety, the distance between you and the vehicle in front should be

Mark one answer

☒ a two-second time gap

☒ one car length

☒ 2 metres (6.6 feet)

☒ two car lengths.

Answer

☒ **a two-second time gap**

One useful method of checking that you've allowed enough room between you and the vehicle in front is the 'Two-Second Rule'.

You should allow a two-second time gap as a safe separation distance. Begin by saying 'Only a fool breaks the Two-Second Rule' when the vehicle in front passes a fixed point. You shouldn't reach that point before you finish saying this. If you do, you're travelling too close and should drop back.

Question

Your overall stopping distance will be much longer when driving

Mark one answer

☒ in the rain

☒ in fog

☒ at night

☒ in strong winds.

Answer

☒ **in the rain**

Extra care should be taken in wet weather. Wet roads will affect the time it takes you to stop. Your stopping distance could be at least doubled.

Question

On a wet road what is the safest way to stop?

Mark one answer

☒ Change gear without braking.

☒ Use the back brake only.

☒ Use the front brake only.

☒ Use both brakes.

Answer

☒ **Use both brakes.**

Motorcyclists need to take extra care when stopping on wet road surfaces. Plan well ahead so that you're able to brake in good time. You should

• ensure your machine is upright

• apply greater pressure to the front brake

• brake when travelling in a straight line.

Question
Road surface is very important to motorcyclists. Which FOUR of these are more likely to reduce the stability of your machine?

Mark four answers

☒ Pot-holes.

☒ Drain covers.

☒ Concrete.

☒ Oil patches.

☒ Tarmac.

☒ Loose gravel.

Answers

☒ **Pot-holes.**

☒ **Drain covers.**

☒ **Oil patches.**

☒ **Loose gravel.**

Apart from the weather conditions, the road surface can affect the stability of a motorcycle. Any change in the road surface can affect the stability of your motorcycle. Be on the lookout for poor road surfaces.

Question
What is the main reason why your stopping distance is longer after heavy rain?

Mark one answer

☒ You may not be able to see large puddles.

☒ The brakes will be cold because they're wet.

☒ Your tyres will have less grip on the road.

☒ Water on the windscreen will blur your view of the road ahead.

Answer

☒ **Your tyres will have less grip on the road.**

When the roads are wet the water will reduce your tyres' grip on the road. When the tyres lose their grip you lose control.

You can cause the tyres to lose their grip by

- excessive acceleration (wheelspin)
- cornering too fast
- braking too hard
- harsh steering (swerving).

Question
You are riding in town. The roads are wet following rain. The reflections from wet surfaces will

Mark one answer

☒ make it easy to see unlit objects

☒ help you to make progress

☒ make it hard to see unlit objects

☒ affect your stopping distance.

Answer

☒ **make it hard to see unlit objects**

If you can't see clearly, slow down and stop. Make sure that your visor or goggles are clean.

Be extra cautious in these conditions.

Question

You are driving in heavy rain when your steering suddenly becomes very light. To get control again you must

Mark one answer

☒ brake firmly to reduce speed

☒ ease off the accelerator

☒ use the accelerator gently

☒ steer towards a dry part of the road.

Answer

☒ **ease off the accelerator**

If you find that your steering becomes light your tyres are losing their grip on the road. To regain control ease off the accelerator. Don't suddenly steer sharply in any direction.

Question

You are driving in heavy rain. Your steering suddenly becomes very light. You should

Mark one answer

☒ steer towards the side of the road

☒ apply gentle acceleration

☒ brake firmly to reduce speed

☒ ease off the accelerator.

Answer

☒ **ease off the accelerator**

Braking harshly in this situation could cause the tyres to lift off the road surface and the wheels to lock, which will result in loss of control. If your vehicle's fitted with an anti-lock braking system (ABS), and your vehicle starts to slide on the wet road surface, apply maximum force to the brake pedal, maintaining this force.

Question

You are riding in heavy rain when your rear wheel skids as you accelerate. To get control again you must

Mark one answer

☒ change down to a lower gear

☒ ease off the throttle

☒ brake to reduce speed

☒ put your feet down.

Answer

☒ **ease off the throttle**

If you feel your back wheel beginning to skid as you pull away ease off the throttle. This will give your rear tyre the chance to grip the road and stop the skid.

Bike skidding to the left

Direction of steering to correct skid

• Ease off brake
• Steer to left

Question
You have driven through a flood. What is the first thing you should do?

Mark one answer

☒ Stop and check the tyres.

☒ Stop and dry the brakes.

☒ Switch on your windscreen wipers.

☒ Test your brakes.

Answer

☒ **Test your brakes.**

After passing through a flood or ford test your brakes. Before you do so make sure that you check behind for following traffic. Don't brake sharply. The vehicle behind may not be able to stop quickly. If necessary, signal your intentions.

Question
You are driving along a country road. You see this sign. AFTER dealing safely with the hazard you should always

Mark one answer

☒ check your tyre pressures

☒ switch on your hazard warning lights

☒ switch on your rear fog lamps

☒ test your brakes.

Answer

☒ **test your brakes**

Deep water can affect your brakes so you should check that they're working properly before you build up speed again. Check your mirrors and consider what's behind you before you do this.

Question
Braking distances on ice can be

Mark one answer

☒ twice the normal distance

☒ five times the normal distance

☒ seven times the normal distance

☒ ten times the normal distance.

Answer

☒ **ten times the normal distance**

Thinking, braking and stopping distances will also be affected by icy and snowy weather. You need to take extra care and expect your stopping distance to increase by up to ten times the normal distance.

Question
Freezing conditions will affect the distance it takes you to come to a stop. You should expect stopping distances to increase by up to

Mark one answer
- ☒ two times
- ☒ five times
- ☒ three times
- ☒ ten times.

Answer
☒ **ten times**

You must take the road and weather conditions into account when driving. It will take considerably longer to stop in bad weather.

Question
When driving in icy conditions, the steering becomes light because the tyres

Mark one answer
- ☒ have more grip on the road
- ☒ are too soft
- ☒ are too hard
- ☒ have less grip on the road.

Answer
☒ **have less grip on the road**

In icy conditions the tyres will lose much of their grip on the road. This could result in the steering becoming light. If you ease off the accelerator you should regain some steering control.

Question
You are driving on an icy road. How can you avoid wheelspin?

Mark one answer
- ☒ Drive at a slow speed in as high a gear as possible.
- ☒ Use the handbrake if the wheels start to slip.
- ☒ Brake gently and repeatedly.
- ☒ Drive in a low gear at all times.

Answer
☒ **Drive at a slow speed in as high a gear as possible.**

If you're travelling on an icy road extra caution will be required to avoid any loss of control. You can reduce wheelspin by driving
- at a slow speed
- in as high a gear as possible.

Question
Skidding is mainly caused by

Mark one answer
- ☒ the weather
- ☒ the driver
- ☒ the vehicle
- ☒ the road.

Answer
☒ **the driver**

You should always consider the conditions and drive accordingly.

Question
How can you avoid wheelspin when driving in freezing conditions?

Mark one answer

☒ Stay in first gear all the time.

☒ Put on your handbrake if the wheels begin to slip.

☒ Drive in as high a gear as possible.

☒ Allow the vehicle to coast in neutral.

Answer

☒ **Drive in as high a gear as possible.**

A low gear will cause the wheels to skid and you'll lose control. A high gear with steady accelerator control will help you to maintain some control.

Question
You are driving in freezing conditions. Which TWO should you do when approaching a sharp bend?

Mark two answers

☒ Accelerate into the bend.

☒ Slow down before you reach the bend.

☒ Gently apply your handbrake.

☒ Avoid sudden steering movements.

☒ Position towards the middle of the road.

Answers

☒ **Slow down before you reach the bend.**

☒ **Avoid sudden steering movements.**

When you're approaching a sharp bend and the road is likely to be icy don't

• accelerate into the bend

• apply your handbrake

• coast (hold the clutch down).

These actions could lead to loss of control.

Question
You are driving in freezing conditions. What should you do when approaching a sharp left-hand bend?

Mark two answers

☒ Slow down before you reach the bend.

☒ Gently apply your handbrake.

☒ Firmly use your footbrake.

☒ Coast into the bend.

☒ Avoid sudden steering movements.

Answers

☒ **Slow down before you reach the bend.**

☒ **Avoid sudden steering movements.**

Avoid steering and braking at the same time. In icy conditions it's very important that you constantly assess what's ahead.

Question

When riding in extremely cold conditions what can you do to keep warm?

Mark one answer

☒ Stay close in behind the vehicles in front.

☒ Wear suitable clothing.

☒ Lie flat on the tank.

☒ Put your hands one at a time on the exhaust pipe.

Answer

☒ **Wear suitable clothing.**

Motorcyclists are exposed to the elements and can become very cold when riding in wintry conditions. It's important to keep warm or concentration could be affected. The only way to stay warm is to wear suitable clothing.

If you do find yourself getting cold then stop at a suitable place to warm up.

Question

You are turning left on a slippery road. The back of your vehicle slides to the right. What should you do?

Mark one answer

☒ Brake firmly and not turn the steering wheel.

☒ Steer carefully to the right.

☒ Steer carefully to the left.

☒ Brake firmly and steer to the left.

Answer

☒ **Steer carefully to the right.**

If you're turning and you feel the back of your vehicle slide to one side steer carefully in the same direction that the back is sliding.

Question

You are turning left on a slippery road. The back of your vehicle slides to the right. You should

Mark one answer

☒ brake firmly and not turn the steering wheel

☒ steer carefully to the left

☒ steer carefully to the right

☒ brake firmly and steer to the left.

Answer

☒ **steer carefully to the right**

This should stop the sliding and allow you to regain control. Don't

- use the accelerator
- use the brakes
- use the clutch.

Question

You are braking on a wet road. Your vehicle begins to skid and you do not have anti-lock brakes. What's the first thing you should do?

Mark one answer

☒ Quickly pull up the handbrake.

☒ Push harder on the brake pedal.

☒ Gently use the accelerator.

☒ Release the footbrake fully.

Answer

☒ **Release the footbrake fully.**

If the skid has been caused by braking too hard for the conditions release the brake. This will allow the wheels to turn and so limit the skid.

Skids are much easier to get into than they are to get out of. Prevention is better than cure. Stay alert to the road and weather conditions. Never drive so fast that you can't stop within the distance that you can see to be clear.

Question

You are braking on a wet road. Your vehicle begins to skid. Your vehicle does not have anti-lock brakes. What is the FIRST thing you should do?

Mark one answer

☒ Quickly pull up the handbrake.

☒ Release the footbrake fully.

☒ Push harder on the brake pedal.

☒ Gently use the accelerator.

Answer

☒ **Release the footbrake fully.**

Many modern vehicles are fitted with anti-lock brakes (ABS). This is a system that senses when the wheels are about to lock under braking. The system releases and reapplies the brakes very quickly, to prevent the wheels locking. Although this reduces the risk of skidding it doesn't relieve the driver of the need to drive with care.

Question

How can you tell when you are driving over black ice?

Mark one answer

☒ It is easier to brake.

☒ The noise from your tyres sounds louder.

☒ You see black ice on the road.

☒ Your steering feels light.

Answer

☒ **Your steering feels light.**

Sometimes you may not be able to see that the road is icy. Black ice makes a road look damp. The signs that you're travelling on black ice can be

• the steering feels light

• the noise from your tyres suddenly goes quiet.

Rear of car skids to the right   **Driver steers to the right**

Question

Coasting the vehicle

Mark one answer

☒ improves the driver's control

☒ makes steering easier

☒ reduces the driver's control

☒ uses more fuel.

Answer

☒ **reduces the driver's control**

'Coasting' is the term used when the clutch is held down and the vehicle is freewheeling. This reduces the driver's control of the vehicle. When you coast the engine can't drive the wheels or hold the car back.

Question

When driving in snow it is best to keep in as high a gear as possible. Why is this?

Mark one answer

- [ ] To help you slow down quickly when you brake.
- [ ] So that wheelspin does not cause your engine to run too fast.
- [ ] To leave a lower gear available in case of wheelspin.
- [ ] To help to prevent wheelspin.

Answer

❌ **To help to prevent wheelspin.**

If the ground is covered in snow move off in as high a gear as possible. Stay in the highest gear you can. This reduces the power to the wheels and so lessens the chance of skidding.

Question

When driving in fog in daylight you should use

Mark one answer

- [ ] sidelights
- [ ] full beam headlights
- [ ] hazard lights
- [ ] dipped headlights.

Answer

❌ **dipped headlights**

Don't drive in fog unless you really have to. Use dipped headlights during daylight. If the visibility is below 100 metres (330 feet) use fog lights and high-intensity rear lights. Let other road users know that you're there.

Question

You're at a junction with limited visibility. You should

Mark one answer

- [ ] inch forward, looking to the right
- [ ] inch forward, looking to the left
- [ ] inch forward, looking both ways
- [ ] be ready to move off quickly.

Answer

❌ **inch forward, looking both ways**

At some road junctions you might find that you can't see clearly into the road that you're joining. Before you commit yourself you have to inch foward, looking both ways. Only emerge when you can see that it's safe to do so. Don't

- speed out hoping the way will be clear
- look one way only.

Question

Why should you ride with a dipped headlamp on in the daytime?

Mark one answer

- [ ] It helps other road users to see you.
- [ ] It means that you can ride faster.
- [ ] Other vehicles will get out of the way.
- [ ] So that it is already on when it gets dark.

Answer

❌ **It helps other road users to see you.**

Your life could depend on being seen clearly.

Question

In very hot weather the road surface can get soft. Which TWO of the following will be affected most?

Mark two answers

☒ The suspension.

☒ The steering.

☒ Braking.

☒ The windscreen.

Answers

☒ The steering.

☒ Braking.

Take care when braking or cornering. Tyres don't grip well on soft tarmac.

Question

In very hot weather the road surface can get soft. Which TWO of the following will be affected most?

Mark two answers

☒ The suspension.

☒ The grip of the tyres.

☒ Braking.

☒ The exhaust.

Answers

☒ The grip of the tyres.

☒ Braking.

Only a small part of your motorcycle's tyres are in contact with the road. This is why you must consider and respect the surface you're on.

Question

You are riding in very hot weather. What are TWO effects that melting tar has on the control of your machine?

Mark two answers

☒ It can make the surface slippery.

☒ It can reduce tyre grip.

☒ It can reduce stopping distances.

☒ It can improve braking efficiency.

Answers

☒ It can make the surface slippery.

☒ It can reduce tyre grip.

In hot weather never be tempted to ride without protective clothing. If you fall from your machine you'll have no protection from the road surface.

Question

Where are you most likely to be affected by a crosswind?

Mark one answer

☒ On a narrow country lane.

☒ On an open stretch of road.

☒ On a busy stretch of road.

☒ On a long, straight road.

Answer

☒ On an open stretch of road.

In windy conditions care must be taken on exposed roads. A strong gust of wind can blow you off course. Watch out for other road users, who may be affected more than you, such as

- cyclists
- motorcyclists
- high-sided lorries
- vehicles towing trailers.

Question

In windy conditions you need to take extra care when

Mark one answer

☒ using the brakes

☒ making a hill start

☒ turning into a narrow road

☒ passing pedal cyclists.

Answer

☒ **passing pedal cyclists**

You should **always** give cyclists plenty of room when overtaking. When it's windy a sudden gust could blow them off course.

Question

Your indicators may be difficult to see in bright sunlight. What should you do?

Mark one answer

☒ Put your indicator on earlier.

☒ Give an arm signal as well as using your indicator.

☒ Touch the brake several times to show the stop lamp.

☒ Turn as quickly as you can.

Answer

☒ **Give an arm signal as well as using your indicator.**

You should always ensure that other road users are aware of your intentions. If you feel your indicator might not be seen then give an arm signal as well.

Question

What should you do to help you see at night?

Mark one answer

☒ Allow a gap beneath your visor or goggles.

☒ Keep your visor or goggles clean.

☒ Wear a tinted visor or goggles.

☒ Don't use a visor or goggles at all.

Answer

☒ **Keep your visor or goggles clean.**

If you're riding a motorcycle at night it's important that you can see clearly. Keep your visor or goggles clean and without smears. Don't wear a tinted visor or goggles at night.

Question

You are riding at night. To be seen more easily, you should

Mark two answers

☒ ride with your headlight on dipped beam

☒ wear reflective clothing

☒ keep the motorcycle clean

☒ stay well out to the right

☒ wear fluorescent clothing.

Answers

☒ **ride with your headlight on dipped beam**

☒ **wear reflective clothing**

Reflective clothing works by reflecting light from the headlights of the other vehicles. This will make it easier for you to be seen. Fluorescent clothing, although effective during the day, won't show up as well at night.

Question

When riding at night you should

Mark two answers

☒ ride with your headlight on dipped beam

☒ wear reflective clothing

☒ wear a tinted visor

☒ ride in the centre of the road

☒ give arm signals.

Answer

☒ **ride with your headlight on dipped beam**

☒ **wear reflective clothing**

Fluorescent clothing shows up in daylight, but at night you should wear reflective clothing. This could be a tabard or reflective body strap.

Question

You are about to go down a steep hill. To control the speed of your vehicle you should

Mark one answer

☒ select a high gear and use the brakes carefully

☒ select a high gear and use the brakes firmly

☒ select a low gear and use the brakes carefully

☒ select a low gear and avoid using the brakes.

Answer

☒ **select a low gear and use the brakes carefully**

When travelling down a steep hill your vehicle will tend to increase speed. This will also make it more difficult for you to stop. To maintain control and prevent the vehicle running away

• select a lower gear – the engine will then help to control your speed

• use the brakes carefully.

Question

You are on a long, downhill slope. What should you do to help control the speed of your vehicle?

Mark one answer

☒ Grip the steering wheel tightly.

☒ Select neutral.

☒ Select a low gear.

☒ Put the clutch down.

Answer

☒ **Select a low gear.**

Selecting a low gear when travelling downhill will help you to control your speed. The engine will assist the brakes and prevent your vehicle gathering speed.

Question

You wish to park facing DOWNHILL. Which TWO of the following should you do?

Mark two answers

☒ Turn the steering wheel towards the kerb.

☒ Park close to the bumper of another car.

☒ Park with two wheels on the kerb.

☒ Put the handbrake on firmly.

☒ Turn the steering wheel away from the kerb.

Answers

☒ **Turn the steering wheel towards the kerb.**

☒ **Put the handbrake on firmly.**

The kerb will stop any forward movement of the vehicle.

Question

You are driving in a built-up area. You approach a speed hump. You should

Mark one answer

☒ move across to the left-hand side of the road

☒ wait for any pedestrians to cross

☒ slow your vehicle right down

☒ stop and check both pavements.

Answer

☒ **slow your vehicle right down**

Many towns have speed humps to slow down traffic. They're often where there are pedestrians, so

• slow right down when driving over them

• they might affect your steering and suspension if you drive too fast

• look out for pedestrians.

Question

When approaching a right-hand bend you should keep well to the left. Why is this?

Mark one answer

- [ ] It improves your view of the road.
- [ ] To overcome the effect of the road's slope.
- [ ] It lets faster traffic from behind overtake.
- [ ] To be positioned safely if the vehicle skids.

Question

You are coming up to a right-hand bend. You should

Mark one answer

- [ ] keep well to the left as it makes the bend faster
- [ ] keep well to the left for a better view around the bend
- [ ] keep well to the right to avoid anything in the gutter
- [ ] keep well to the right to make the bend less sharp.

Answer

✗ It improves your view of the road.

Don't

- move over to the right to try and straighten the bend. You could endanger yourself by getting too close to oncoming traffic.
- cross or straddle unbroken white lines along the centre of the road
- drive so fast that you can't stop within your range of vision.

Answer

✗ keep well to the left for a better view around the bend

There could be a hazard just around the bend. Always be aware of this and you'll be better prepared to deal with it if you need to.

SECTION 5 HAZARD AWARENESS

This section looks at judgement and hazard perception.

The questions will ask you about

- anticipation

- hazard awareness

- attention

- speed and distance

- reaction time

- the effects of alcohol and drugs

- tiredness.

Question
You see this sign on the rear of a slow–moving lorry that you want to pass. It is travelling in the middle of the road. You should

Mark one answer

☒ cautiously approach the lorry then pass on either side

☒ follow the lorry until you can leave the motorway

☒ wait on the hard shoulder until the lorry has stopped

☒ approach with care and keep to the left of the lorry.

Question
Where would you expect to see these markers?

Mark two answers

☒ On a motorway sign.

☒ At the entrance to a narrow bridge.

☒ On a large goods vehicle.

☒ On a builder's skip placed on the road.

Answer

☒ **approach with care and keep to the left of the lorry**

This sign indicates that you should keep to the left of the vehicle. If you wish to overtake then you should do so on the left. Be aware that there might be workmen in the area.

Answers

☒ **On a large goods vehicle.**

☒ **On a builder's skip placed on the road.**

These markers are reflective so that they show up at night. If you see them ahead then you should be aware that there might be a stationary, slow or long vehicle.

Question

What does this signal, from a police officer, mean to oncoming traffic?

Mark one answer

- ☒ Go ahead.
- ☒ Stop.
- ☒ Turn left.
- ☒ Turn right.

Answer

☒ Stop.

Police officers might be found at a point where there's heavy traffic or a breakdown of traffic lights. Check your *Highway Code* for the signals that they use.

Question

What is the main hazard shown in this picture?

Mark one answer

- ☒ Vehicles turning right.
- ☒ Vehicles doing U-turns.
- ☒ The cyclist crossing the road.
- ☒ Parked cars around the corner.

Answer

☒ The cyclist crossing the road.

Look at the picture carefully and try to imagine you're there.

The cyclist in this picture isn't crossing the road in the correct place. You must be able to deal with the unexpected, especially when you're planning your approach to a hazardous junction. There will be several things to think about on your approach so look well ahead to give yourself time to deal with them.

Question
Which road user has caused a hazard?

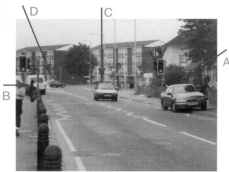

Mark one answer

- ☒ The parked car (arrowed A).
- ☒ The pedestrian waiting to cross (arrowed B).
- ☒ The moving car (arrowed C).
- ☒ The car turning (arrowed D).

Answer

☒ **The parked car (arrowed A).**

The car has parked on the approach to a pedestrian crossing. The road is marked with white zigzag lines. Don't park on these – they're there for a reason. Parking here will

- block the view for pedestrians wishing to cross the road
- restrict the view of the crossing for traffic approaching.

Question
When approaching a hazard your FIRST reaction should be to

Mark one answer

- ☒ use your footbrake
- ☒ change direction
- ☒ release the accelerator
- ☒ check the mirrors.

Answer

 ☒ **check the mirrors**

Look well ahead and around so that you're as ready as possible for hazards that occur. Be aware of what's behind you. You might need to indicate that you're slowing down or changing direction.

Question

What should the driver of the car approaching the crossing do?

Mark one answer

- ☒ Continue at the same speed.
- ☒ Sound the horn.
- ☒ Drive through quickly.
- ☒ Slow down and get ready to stop.

Answer

☒ **Slow down and get ready to stop.**

Look well ahead to see if any hazards are developing. This will give you more time to deal with them in the correct way. The man in the picture is clearly intending to cross the road. You should be travelling at a speed that allows you to check your mirror, slow down and stop in good time. You shouldn't have to brake harshly.

Question

What should the driver of the red car do?

Mark one answer

- ☒ Wave the pedestrians who are waiting to cross.
- ☒ Wait for the pedestrian in the road to cross.
- ☒ Quickly drive behind the pedestrian in the road.
- ☒ Tell the pedestrian in the road she should not have crossed.

Answer

☒ **Wait for the pedestrian in the road to cross.**

Some people might take longer to cross the road. They may be elderly or have a disability. Be patient and don't hurry them by showing your impatience. They might have poor eyesight or not be able to hear traffic approaching.

Don't signal or wave the pedestrian to cross the road. Other road users may not have seen your signal and this could lead the pedestrian into a hazardous situation.

Question
What THREE things should the driver of the grey car be specially aware of?

Mark three answers

☒ Pedestrians stepping out between cars.

☒ The bumpy road surface.

☒ Empty parking spaces.

☒ Other cars behind the grey car.

☒ Cars leaving parking spaces.

☒ Parked cars' doors opening.

Answers

☒ **Pedestrians stepping out between cars.**

☒ **Cars leaving parking spaces.**

☒ **Parked cars' doors opening.**

Your awareness in hazardous situations is very important. In a busy street like the one in the picture there are many potential dangers. You might not be able to see a pedestrian crossing from between the parked vehicles. A driver or passenger of a parked car might open a door.

Drive or ride at a speed that will allow you to stop in good time if a hazard suddenly appears. It could happen at any time.

Question
What should the driver of the red car (arrowed) do?

Mark one answer

☒ Sound the horn to tell other drivers where he is.

☒ Squeeze through the gap.

☒ Wave the driver of the white car to go on.

☒ Wait until the car blocking the way has moved.

Answer

☒ **Wait until the car blocking the way has moved.**

If you're moving in slow-moving traffic think ahead so that you don't block junctions or stop others' progress. Don't

• force others to give way to you

• sound the horn to gain priority

• flash your lights to gain or give prority

• give any other misleading signal.

Question

What should the driver of the grey car (arrowed) do?

Mark one answer

- ☒ Cross if the way is clear.
- ☒ Reverse out of the box junction.
- ☒ Wait in the same place until the lights are green.
- ☒ Wait until the lights are red then cross.

Answer

☒ **Cross if the way is clear.**

Yellow markings are marked on the road to prevent busy junctions becoming blocked with traffic. Don't enter the box unless your exit road is clear.

When turning right you can wait in the box if your exit road is clear but you can't proceed due to the oncoming traffic.

Question

What should the driver of a car coming up to this level crossing do?

Mark one answer

- ☒ Drive through quickly.
- ☒ Drive through carefully.
- ☒ Stop before the barrier.
- ☒ Switch on hazard warning lights.

Answer

☒ **Stop before the barrier.**

Approach and cross level crossings with care. If you need to stop, wait patiently. In this picture there's a junction on the left, before the crossing; keep clear of the defined road markings. Don't

- try to beat the barrier by driving through
- drive or ride onto the crossing unless the road is clear on the other side
- drive or ride nose-to-tail over it
- stop on or just over the crossing.

Question

What are TWO main hazards a driver should be aware of when driving along this street?

Mark two answers

- ☒ Glare from the sun.
- ☒ Car doors opening suddenly.
- ☒ Lack of road markings.
- ☒ The headlights on parked cars being switched on.
- ☒ Large goods vehicles.
- ☒ Children running out from between vehicles.

Answers

- ☒ **Car doors opening suddenly.**
- ☒ **Children running out from between vehicles.**

When driving or riding on roads where there are many parked vehicles you must take extra care. Always be ready for the unexpected and drive or ride accordingly.

Children are small and you might not be able to see them about to emerge from between cars. Drivers may be getting in and out of their vehicles, providing another potential hazard. If the road is narrow, as it is in this picture, you'll also need to look well down the road. This will help you to deal with any oncoming traffic safely.

Question

What is the main hazard a driver should be aware of when following this cyclist?

Mark one answer

- ☒ The cyclist may move into the left gap and dismount.
- ☒ The cyclist may swerve out into the road.
- ☒ The contents of the cyclist's carrier may fall onto the road.
- ☒ The cyclist may wish to turn right at the end of the road.

Answer

- ☒ **The cyclist may swerve out into the road.**

When following a cyclist be aware that they also have to deal with the hazards around them. They may wobble or swerve to avoid a pot-hole in the road. They might see a potential hazard and change direction suddenly.

Don't drive or ride very close to them or rev your engine impatiently. This will only add to their perception of a hazard and may rush them into a dangerous decision.

Question

The driver of which car has caused a hazard?

Mark one answer

- ☒ Car A.
- ☒ Car B.
- ☒ Car C.
- ☒ Car D.

Question

You think the driver of the vehicle in front has forgotten to cancel his right indicator. You should

Mark one answer

- ☒ sound your horn before overtaking
- ☒ overtake on the left if there's room
- ☒ flash your lights to alert the driver
- ☒ stay behind and not overtake.

Answer

☒ **Car A.**

The driver of car A has forced the approaching vehicle to the right onto the hatch-marked area of the road. It's also blocked the view of the other vehicle trying to emerge.

When dealing with busy junctions consider the other road users around you. Your actions must not put any other driver or rider at risk.

Answer

☒ **stay behind and not overtake**

The driver may be unsure of the location of a junction and suddenly turn. Be cautious.

Question

What is the main hazard the driver of the red car (arrowed) should be most aware of?

Answer

❌ The bus may move out into the road.

You should try to anticipate the actions of the other road users around you. The driver of the red car should have made a mental note that the bus was at the bus stop. If you do this you'll be prepared for the bus pulling out. Look and see how many more passengers are waiting to board. If the last one has just got on, the bus is likely to move off.

Mark one answer

❌ Glare from the sun may affect the driver's vision.

❌ The black car may stop suddenly.

❌ The bus may move out into the road.

❌ Oncoming vehicles will assume the driver is turning right.

Question

In heavy motorway traffic you're being followed closely by the vehicle behind. How can you lower the risk of an accident?

Answer

❌ Increase your distance from the vehicle in front.

On a busy motorway, traffic might still travel at high speeds although the weight of traffic means the vehicles are close together. Don't follow too close to the vehicle in front. If a driver behind seems to be 'pushing' you, increase your distance from the car in front by easing off the accelerator. This will lessen the risk of an accident involving several vehicles.

Mark one answer

❌ Increase your distance from the vehicle in front.

❌ Tap your foot on the brake pedal.

❌ Switch on your hazard lights.

❌ Move onto the hard shoulder and stop.

Question

To drive you must be able to read a number plate from what distance?

Mark one answer

☒ 10 metres (33 feet).

☒ 15 metres (50 feet).

☒ 20.5 metres (67 feet).

☒ 205 metres (673 feet).

Answer

 20.5 metres (67 feet).

When you take your practical test your examiner will ask you to read a number plate from a distance of 20.5 metres (67 feet). This is a legal requirement to ensure that you see situations around you on the road.

Question

You find that you need glasses to read vehicle number plates. When must you wear them?

Mark one answer

☒ Only in bad weather conditions.

☒ At all times when driving.

☒ Only when you think it necessary.

☒ Only in bad light or at night time.

Answer

 At all times when driving.

Have your eyesight tested before you start your practical training. Then, throughout your driving life, have periodical checks to ensure that your eyes haven't deteriorated.

Question

A driver can only read a number plate at the required distance with glasses on. The glasses should be worn

Mark one answer

☒ all the time when driving

☒ only when driving long distances

☒ only when reversing

☒ only in poor visibility.

Answer

☒ **all the time when driving**

You might find you need glasses or contact lenses to read number plates. This is fine, but you must then wear them when you drive or ride.

Question

You're about to drive home. You can't find the glasses you need to wear when driving. You should

Mark one answer

☒ drive home slowly, keeping to quiet roads

☒ borrow a friend's glasses and drive home

☒ drive home at night, so that the lights will help you

☒ find a way of getting home without driving.

Answer

 find a way of getting home without driving

Don't be tempted to drive if you've lost or forgotten your glasses. It's an obvious statement that you must be able to see clearly when driving.

Question

Which THREE result from drinking alcohol and driving?

Mark three answers

☒ Less control.

☒ A false sense of confidence.

☒ Faster reactions.

☒ Poor judgement of speed.

☒ Greater awareness of danger.

Answers

☒ **Less control.**

☒ **A false sense of confidence.**

☒ **Poor judgement of speed.**

From the start you must understand the dangers of mixing alcohol with driving or riding. One drink is too many if you're going to drive or ride. Alcohol will reduce your ability to drive or ride safely.

Question

What are THREE ways that drinking alcohol can affect driving?

Mark three answers

☒ It slows down your reactions.

☒ It reduces your co-ordination.

☒ It affects your judgement of speed.

☒ It reduces your confidence.

Answers

☒ **It slows down your reactions.**

☒ **It reduces your co-ordination.**

☒ **It affects your judgement of speed.**

Drivers who drink before driving or riding are responsible for numerous deaths on our roads. One death is too many.

Question

Which THREE of these are likely effects of drinking alcohol on driving?

Mark three answers

☒ Reduced co-ordination.

☒ Increased confidence.

☒ Poor judgement.

☒ Increased concentration.

☒ Faster reactions.

☒ Colour blindness.

Answers

☒ **Reduced co-ordination.**

☒ **Increased confidence.**

☒ **Poor judgement.**

Alcohol can increase confidence to a point where a driver or rider's behaviour might become 'out of character'. Someone who normally behaves sensibly suddenly takes risks and enjoys it. Never let yourself or your friends get into this situation.

Question

How does alcohol affect your driving?

Mark one answer

☒ It speeds up your reactions.

☒ It increases your awareness.

☒ It improves your co-ordination.

☒ It reduces your concentration.

Answer

✖ **It reduces your concentration.**

Concentration and good judgement at all times are needed to be a good, safe driver.

Question

When driving, what is the maximum **legal** level for alcohol in your blood?

Mark one answer

☒ 50 mg per 100 ml.

☒ 60 mg per 100 ml.

☒ 80 mg per 100 ml.

☒ 90 mg per 100 ml.

Answer

✖ **80 mg per 100 ml.**

The maximum legal level for alcohol in your blood is 80 mg per 100 ml.

By the time you get to know how much alcohol you have in your blood it may be too late. It will probably mean that you've been asked to give a sample to the police.

Question

The maximum prison sentence for the offence of driving while unfit through drink and drugs is

Mark one answer

☒ 12 months

☒ 18 months

☒ six months

☒ 24 months.

Answer

✖ **six months**

The results of an accident through drinking touch many people, not just those physically involved. Relationships, careers, ambitions can be ruined. Think of what might happen. Don't drink if you're going to drive.

Question

Which one of the following IS NOT affected by alcohol?

Mark one answer

☒ Judgement of speed.

☒ Reaction time.

☒ Perception of colours.

☒ Co-ordination.

Answer

✖ **Perception of colours.**

If you're going out, and intend to drive or ride, the safest option is to not drink alcohol at all. Enjoy yourself, but if you do drink, don't drive or ride.

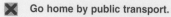

Question

What advice should you give to a driver who has had a few alcoholic drinks at a party?

Mark one answer

☒ Have a strong cup of coffee and then drive home.

☒ Drive home carefully and slowly.

☒ Wait a short while and then drive home.

☒ Go home by public transport.

Answer

☒ **Go home by public transport.**

Drinking black coffee or waiting a few hours won't make any difference. Alcohol takes time to leave the body. You might even be unfit to drive or ride the following morning.

Question

A driver attends a social event. What precaution should the driver take?

Mark one answer

☒ Drink plenty of coffee after drinking alcohol.

☒ Avoid busy roads after drinking alcohol.

☒ Avoid drinking alcohol completely.

☒ Avoid drinking alcohol on an empty stomach.

Answer

 Avoid drinking alcohol completely.

This is always going to be the safest option. One drink could be too many.

Question

Your doctor has given you a course of medicine. Why should you ask if it is OK to drive?

Mark one answer

☒ Drugs make you a better driver by quickening your reactions.

☒ You'll have to let your insurance company know about the medicine.

☒ Some types of medicine can cause your reactions to slow down.

☒ The medicine you take may affect your hearing.

Answer

☒ **Some types of medicine can cause your reactions to slow down.**

Always check the label of any medication container. The contents might affect your driving. If you aren't sure, ask your doctor or pharmacist.

Question

The offence of causing death whilst driving under the influence of drink or drugs carries the maximum penalty of

Mark one answer

☒ eight years' imprisonment

☒ ten years' imprisonment

☒ 12 years' imprisonment

☒ six years' imprisonment.

Answer

 ten years' imprisonment

Think about this when someone offers you a drink and you have your car with you. Drinking and driving can ruin your life as well as damage others'.

Question

You are not sure if your cough medicine will affect your driving. What TWO things could you do?

Mark two answers

☒ Ask your doctor.

☒ Check the medicine label.

☒ Drive if you feel alright.

☒ Ask a friend or relative for advice.

Answers

☒ **Ask your doctor.**

☒ **Check the medicine label.**

If you're taking medicine or drugs prescribed by your doctor check to ensure that they won't make you drowsy. If you forget to ask at the time of your visit to the surgery, check with your pharmacist.

Question

You take some cough medicine given to you by a friend. What must you do before driving?

Mark one answer

☒ Drink some strong coffee.

☒ Ask your friend if taking the medicine affected their driving.

☒ Check the label to see if the medicine will affect your driving.

☒ Make a short journey to see if the medicine's affecting your driving.

Answer

☒ **Check the label to see if the medicine will affect your driving.**

Never drive or ride having taken drugs you don't know about. They might affect your judgement and perception, and therefore endanger lives.

Question

You have taken medication that may make you feel drowsy. Your friends tell you it is safe to drive. What should you do?

Mark one answer

☒ Take their advice and drive.

☒ Ignore your friends' advice and do not drive.

☒ Only drive if they come with you.

☒ Drive for short distances only.

Answer

☒ **Ignore your friends' advice and do not drive.**

Friends may have their own reasons for wanting you to drive. Don't take the risk: it's never worth it.